OCKERMOUTH

Egypt

The Living Past

Egypt
The Living Past

TGH James

Photographs by Graham Harrison

British Museum Press
in association with the
Egyptian State Information Service

Text © 1992 T.G.H. James
Photographs © 1992 Graham Harrison
Published by British Museum Press
A division of British Museum Publications Ltd
46 Bloomsbury Street, London WC1B 3QQ

British Library Cataloguing in Publication Data
James, T.G.H.
  Egypt : Living Past
  I. Title
  932

ISBN 0-7141-0963-0

Designed by Paul Ryan
Printed in Hong Kong

Frontispiece. One of the lady guests at the
funeral banquet depicted in the tomb
 of Ramose, vizier of Egypt in the reigns of
Amenophis III and Amenophis IV
(*c.* 1355-1350 BC).
This page. The pyramids of Giza, viewed
across the desert escarpment (Fourth
Dynasty, *c.* 2540-2470 BC).

In memory of
MAGDI WAHBA
with whom so many of the themes in this book
were discussed over more than forty years

Contents

Photographic   Acknowledgements

Taking the photographs which illustrate this book would not have been possible without the enthusiasm and support of many people. However, thanks must go primarily to Celia Clear, Publishing Manager of British Museum Press, whose idea the book was; to Teresa Francis, editor; Julie Young, production manager; and Paul Ryan, the book's designer.

For the invaluable assistance provided throughout Egypt, grateful thanks must be extended to Dr Mamdouh El Beltagui, Chairman of the Egyptian State Information Service (SIS). Thanks are also due to Dr Ali A. Rahmy, Director of the Press and Information Bureau, Embassy of Egypt, London; Ahmed Al-Ibrashy, Director of the Cairo International Press Centre; and Ahmed Nasr Said, Press Attaché, Press and Information Bureau, Embassy of Egypt, London.

For their dedication and hard work, a special note of appreciation must go to Ahmad Nagaty, Mrs Sohair Hussien, Abdou Hassan, Mrs Nagwa Bakir and Mrs Laïla Soliman of the Cairo International Press Centre; and Ahmed Nouby Moussa of SIS Luxor; Houssien Mokhtar, SIS Abu Simbel; Hosny Mohamed Hassan, SIS Alexandria; Ezzat Emam Gamie, SIS El Dakhla; Mohamed Fathi Ali El Saie, SIS Mallawi; and Anwar Mohamed Abd El Hafez and Ali Mohamed Ali of SIS El Kharga.

Thanks are also due to Mohamed Khlil Abou Zeid, Salah Abo Al Saaud, Mohamed Hussien, Farag Towfik, Abou El Fath El Safty, Samira Abd El Mak Soud and Mrs Madiha Nawar of the SIS; Ahmed Abdel Hadi, Ahmed Lutfi, Gamal Hussien Hamdy and Mohamed Magdy Daif of the Cairo International Press Centre; Hala Abdel Wahab of the TV Centre, Cairo; Tarek Hassanien of the Suez Canal Authority; and Mohamed Aly Heida of Siwa Oasis.

For their kindness, thanks must also go to Sheikh Mahmoud Mohamed Abde El Maksood, Islamic leader of the New Valley; Father Sidrack and Father Thadrus of St Bishoi's Monastery; and Father Diuesocorus of St Antony's Monastery.

A mention of appreciation also to SIS drivers Mohamed Ahmed Hassanen, Said Atia Ahmed and Mr Mohamed; to the management and staff of the Windsor Hotel, Cairo; to photographer Fouad Elkoury for his words of wisdom; to Yasin Safadi, Head of the British Library's Arabic section; and finally to Mrs Audrey Harrison for organising everything at home.

Graham Harrison

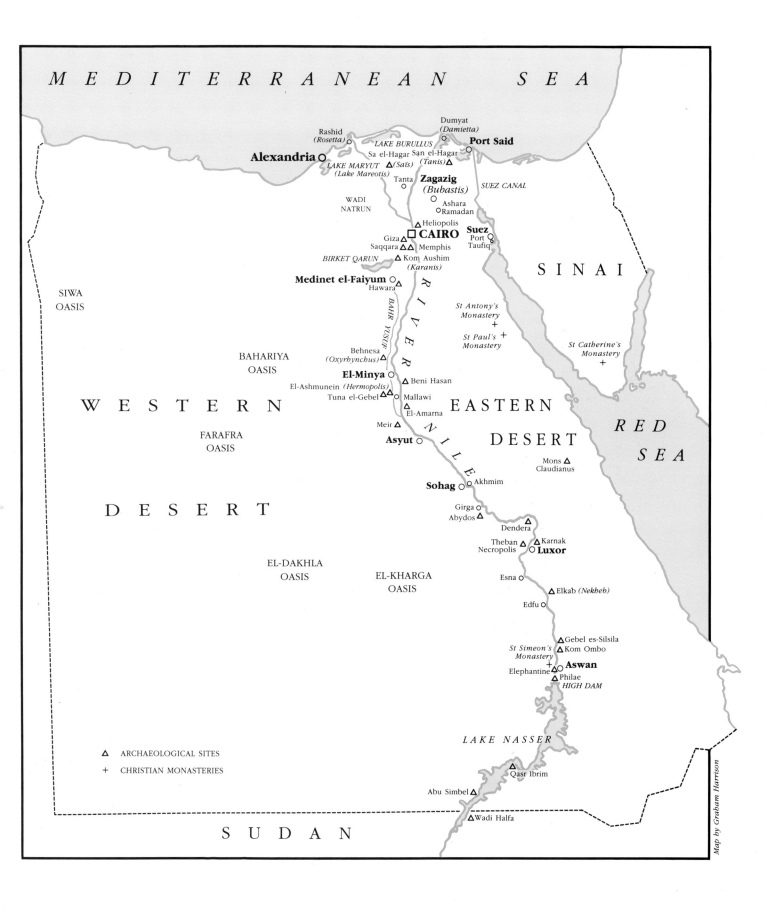

MEDITERRANEAN SEA

Rashid
(Rosetta) ○
Alexandria ○
LAKE MARYUT
(Lake Mareotis)
Dumyat
(Damietta) ○
LAKE BURULLUS
Sa el-Hagar
△ (Sais)
San el-Hagar
(Tanis) △
Port Said ○○
SUEZ CANAL
Tanta ○
Zagazig
(Bubastis)
WADI
NATRUN
Ashara
○ Ramadan
△ Heliopolis
□ CAIRO
Giza △○
Saqqara △△ △ Memphis
Suez ○
Port ○○
Taufiq
SINAI
BIRKET QARUN
△ Kom Aushim
(Karanis)
Medinet el-Faiyum ○△
Hawara
BAHR
YUSIF
RIVER
St Antony's
Monastery
+
St Paul's
Monastery +
St Catherine's
Monastery
+
RED
SEA
SIWA
OASIS
BAHARIYA
OASIS
Behnesa
(Oxyrhynchus)
El-Minya ○
El-Ashmunein (Hermopolis)
Tuna el-Gebel △△
△ Beni Hasan
○ Mallawi
△ El-Amarna
Meir △
Asyut ○
WESTERN
FARAFRA
OASIS
NILE
EASTERN
DESERT
DESERT
Mons △
Claudianus
EL-DAKHLA
OASIS
EL-KHARGA
OASIS
Sohag ○
○ Akhmim
Girga ○
Abydos △
Dendera △
Theban
Necropolis
○ Luxor
△ Karnak
Esna ○
△ Elkab (Nekheb)
Edfu ○
△ Gebel es-Silsila
△ Kom Ombo
St Simeon's
Monastery
+
Elephantine
△○ Aswan
△ Philae
HIGH DAM
LAKE NASSER
△ ARCHAEOLOGICAL SITES
+ CHRISTIAN MONASTERIES
Qasr Ibrim △
Abu Simbel △
△ Wadi Halfa
SUDAN

Map by Graham Harrison

7

The Nile: Bringer of Life

How can one get away from the cliché that the land of Egypt is the creation of the Nile? What Herodotus, the Greek historian, said should be translated more precisely as 'Egypt is the gift of the river', a statement which comes in a passage of generalities about Egypt, written with perspicacity in the fifth century BC and still, for the most part, fitting for the Egypt of the late twentieth century AD:

> For it is clear, even to one who has heard nothing in advance, but uses his eyes, who has understanding, that the Egypt to which the Greeks sail, is for the Egyptians an acquired land, and a gift of the river.... The nature of the land of Egypt is as follows: firstly, if you are sailing, and while still a day's journey from land, you let down a sounding-line, you bring up mud at eleven fathoms in depth. This demonstrates that the discharge of the land extends this far.

There can be few countries in which the effects of invasion, conquest, changes in religion, successive cultural traditions, political vicissitudes, education, literacy, industrialisation, travel and pervasive modernism have been absorbed, and in various ways transmuted, even neutralised, as they have been in Egypt. The land of Egypt still retains a very substantial element of what was observed by the ancient Greek traveller. It would, of course, be foolish to maintain that nothing much has changed in the intervening two and a half millennia; but attitudes of mind, beliefs in religion, practices of skills and craftsmanship and art, perceptions of the natural

1 The Temple of Philae, rebuilt on Agilkia Island in the lake between the old Aswan Dam (seen in the background) and the new High Dam. From the Island of Biga, site of a more ancient shrine and the mythical source of the Nile.

world, can be seen to have profound continuities throughout this time, and these continuities can easily be extended back an equally long way, to the beginning of the First Dynasty. Historians and chroniclers, from very ancient times, have seen the beginnings of Egypt as a unified state in the triumph of the Upper Egyptian king Menes over Lower Egypt in about 3000 BC. The tradition of this act of unification of Upper and Lower Egypt (the Nile Valley and the Delta) goes back initially to the lost compilation of Manetho, an Egyptian priest who systematised Egyptian history in the reign of the Greek king Ptolemy II Philadelphus in about 275 BC. His organisation of the kings of Egypt into dynasties and his narrative framework of political developments over the Dynastic Period, epitomised and preserved by a number of later ancient writers, has in itself provided a powerful thread of continuity in the perception of ancient Egyptian history. There are many hints surviving from the Middle and New Kingdom periods which suggest that Manetho drew on and perpetuated the ancient native perception of the progress of that history.

Herodotus was undoubtedly right to emphasise the geographical factors which for him marked out Egypt as a distinct and peculiar country in the ambit of his world; and of these factors, the primacy of the Nile cannot be denied. Although the crowds of tourists that visit Egypt annually travel principally to see the ancient monuments of the land, they are also attracted by the promise of a very reliable climate and the almost certain presence of the sun. Yet many will return from their brief stay with a pervading impression of water. Egypt is an African country, or, perhaps more precisely, a country in the continent of Africa. Its geographical situation and modern political necessities reinforce the African connection, even though, throughout the millennia, the country and its peoples have usually looked north and east for both political and cultural purposes. The African countries to the south, particularly the Sudan and Ethiopia, have in recent years been devastated by troubled politics and by famine, the latter being the result partly of the former, but more immediately of the failure of the rains. And yet the Sudan and Ethiopia provide the bulk of the water by which Egypt flourishes, the Sudan as the conduit for the White Nile and Ethiopia as the source of the Blue Nile. Egypt's remarkable political stability, fragile though it has been for brief periods since its separation from the Ottoman Empire, may not be the result of the ever-flowing Nile, but it is substantially underpinned by a relative abundance of water.

It is surely not true that there is such a resource of water in Egypt that it can be

2 Waterwheel and water channel in a palm-grove by the Bahr Sinnuris in the Faiyum. Water and its distribution have particular qualities in the Faiyum, where streams and even small waterfalls can be seen.

3 *left* Boat-builders on the frame of a boat in a shipbuilding yard at Rashid (Rosetta), in the Nile estuary on the coast of the Delta.

4 *above* Ankhwa, a boat-builder; a granite statue of the early Old Kingdom (c. 2600 BC) in which the subject is shown holding an adze, the traditional tool of the boat-builder (British Museum, 171).

squandered without regard for sensible economy; yet this is the impression given to the visitor by the lavish way in which lawns and flower beds are drenched in the fertile gardens of the modern hotels outside the centre of Cairo. Memories of summer droughts in Britain are confounded by the constant running of hose-pipes and little irrigation canals, by the lush appearance of turf and shrubberies beneath the baking sun, the like of which would soon bring restrictions of water supply in a northern country where five successive sunny summer days might constitute a heat-wave. The appearance of superabundance is mistaken, and it will not be long before a perceptive visitor will note the attention to water supply which is a perennial concern in Egypt. The balance between plenty and insufficiency, between lush cultivation and a regression to desert, is maintained only by massive control, eternal vigilance and desperate forward planning. With the construction in the 1960s of the great High Dam south of Aswan, at the southern limits of what was conceived as the finite land of Egypt in antiquity, some solutions were found but many unexpected problems were generated for the future. There exists at present, however, a kind of plateau in the Egyptian water economy which was the promised land of those who first considered the new dam even in the days before the revolution of 1952.

This plateau was reached by a slow ascent marked by the successive schemes of water control developed since the late nineteenth century, represented by the remarkable series of barrages across the Nile and dominated by the first great Aswan Dam of 1899 with its successive heightenings up to the 1930s. No one knows, or perhaps can even imagine, what lies beyond the plateau. Will it remain steady, or rise in a gradual way to meet the growing demands for water in a country where the population has risen (without a very substantial increase in the area under cultivation) from about fourteen million in 1900 to almost fifty-five million in 1990? The alternative of a decline in supply, exacerbated by population increases, can scarcely be contemplated with equanimity. And there are other factors which may render the task of Egypt's water engineers and administrators almost impossible in present circumstances. Without giving too much credence to the prophets of ecological disaster through pollution and the so-called greenhouse effect, some attention will have to be paid to the increased requirements of the sadly underprivileged inhabitants of the lands bordering the Nile to the south of Egypt. These peoples have since time immemorial watched the waters of their rivers pass them by; they have used what they wanted, and done nothing much to save this resource for difficult times. The lessons of conservation and exploitation are not difficult to learn, and Egypt can offer the excellent example of how solutions can be reached.

Although the Nile is the most important water source in the Sudan, much of the agriculture there, especially in the west and south of the country, depends on seasonal rains. In Egypt the Nile is central and unique as a source of water for agriculture and all the purposes of daily life. There are subterranean water resources beneath the Western Desert, but they have yet to be seriously investigated; although, as we shall see, they provide the life blood of the distant oases. Wells can be sunk in the Nile Valley itself, but the water they yield is mostly subsoil water of Nile origin and limited in quantity. However, they are useful for limited cultivation and for domestic purposes, and they were especially useful in settlements some distance from the river before the advent of piped supplies. Ancient wells can still be seen in some of the great temples of antiquity, and others can be detected in the city areas of places like El-Amarna, the ancient capital of King Akhenaten. In temples a constant source of water was needed for ritual purposes in the sacred ceremonies. An excellent example of an ancient well, lined with fine masonry and with a convenient but narrow descending stair, served the requirements of the temple of Sobk and Haroeris at Kom Ombo; it still contains water to a considerable depth. The sacred lakes in the great temple of Amon-Re at Karnak and in the neighbouring temple of Mut are also filled by subsoil water and demonstrate admirably the hydraulic principle which allowed their making in antiquity. In the temple of Hathor at Dendera, a good mile and a half from the river, the splendidly constructed lake, which is in fact more of a large tank in the Indian sense, now rarely has water in its bottom but is damp enough to allow a very picturesque and bosky miniature environment to flourish in the arid temple enclosure.

Water for ritual purposes remains important in the religious life of Egypt. Every mosque has its fountain or tank for ritual ablutions, and while this feature is not peculiar to Egypt - think only of Granada or Cordoba - and is specifically Muslim, it is not too fanciful to identify a connection or continuity from ancient times. It was, without a doubt, only a matter of convenience which led to the opportunist use of the great conglomerate coffin of Nectanebo II of the Thirtieth Dynasty as the impressive ablution tank in the Attarine mosque in Alexandria, and previously, possibly, in the church of St Athanasius on the same site. The shape and size of the sarcophagus make it a formidable bath, with holes drilled near the base to let out the water. What a many-layered object of complicated significance! Such an

5 An evening view of the Nile at Aswan at the northern end of the First Cataract. Here, in this rocky region, was the southern boundary of Egypt in antiquity. Aswan still retains the character of a frontier town.

object is an icon of continuity indeed. Someone in the years following the burial of Nectanebo in 341 BC looted the royal tomb and emptied the sarcophagus; later it was moved from Behbeit el-Hagar to Alexandria - all seven tonnes of it - where it was imaginatively recycled in medieval times. What did people think of the multitude of hieroglyphs covering the surfaces? Presumably nothing. A more subtle and meaningful connection might have been made by the ancient Egyptians, for whom the association of royal coffin and water would have suggested the dispatch of Osiris in a coffin by his brother Seth, and its journey by sea to Byblos in the Lebanon.

In the funeral rituals of ancient Egypt the pouring of libations of pure water was essentially both a washing and a gift of life; it was as a requirement of life that water was most appreciated, and it came from the Nile. As with so many other things - objects, creatures, even ideas, natural phenomena, geographical features, heavenly bodies - the ancient Egyptian could treat the Nile both for what it was - a river containing useful water - and as a divine element, or the vehicle for a divine element. The river was there to be used; in addition to being the constant source of water for all daily purposes, it was Egypt's main highway. It offered the easiest and most direct way to travel from one end of the country to the other, a country notable, at least south of the Delta, as a land of all length and very little breadth. A boat in water could travel steadily northwards using the natural flow of the river; in travelling south, against the flow, the convenient and prevailing north wind could fill the boat's sails. The buoyant qualities of water could support almost any weight of cargo to be transported over daunting distances; the absence of the river would have greatly hampered the building of vast stone structures and inhibited the development of the extraordinary ancient activities of quarrying and working very hard stones - granites, schist, basalt, quartzite.

Although the main building stones of antiquity, used in the erection of the structures 'for eternity' (as the Egyptians said), were limestone and sandstone, the harder stones, particularly granite, were employed for special constructional features in great tombs and temples. Characteristically, the Great Pyramid of Cheops at Giza was one of the first to incorporate granite in its building: the king's burial chamber is made entirely of granite, the roof consisting of nine slabs estimated as weighing together about 400 tonnes. These great blocks had to be brought from quarries at Aswan, about 530 miles to the south by river. The great funerary temple of Queen Hatshepsut, built over one thousand years later, has a scene which

explicitly shows the transport of two granite obelisks from Aswan to Karnak - admittedly a journey of only 65 miles - and the presence of granite obelisks from Aswan at Karnak and Luxor demonstrates that the scene was neither imaginary nor inaccurate. Huge masses of stone, whether in single monumental pieces or as cargoes of building blocks, were regularly conveyed by river. Of course, the problem of transport was relatively simple once the necessary load had been stowed securely on its boat or barge; five miles or five hundred miles were possible on a river that in normal circumstances offered few hazards to the captain of a boat other than the mud-banks and attendant shallows which changed season by season.

The real problems lay in bringing the great stones to the water's edge, loading them without damage, and ultimately reversing the sequence at the point of destination. It is difficult to resist the dry account Belzoni gave of his first attempt to load the obelisk from Philae, a relatively modest monument of about seven metres in length, for transport north in 1818. A jetty had been built to facilitate the move from land to boat:

> …the pier appeared quite strong enough to bear at least forty times the weight it had to support; but, alas! when the obelisk came gradually on from the sloping bank, and all the weight rested on it, the pier, with the obelisk, and some of the men, took a slow movement, and majestically descended into the river, wishing us better success.

In retrospect Belzoni could treat the matter rather lightly, for at second go he was successful. What would have happened three thousand years ago if - indeed when - such an accident occurred? Our relatively sparse records from antiquity make no mention of such mishaps, but high officials were not averse from boasting when great projects, and especially quarrying activities, were carried through to the complete satisfaction of His Majesty. Success must imply occasional failure.

The Nile remained the most important artery of communication in Egypt up until thirty years ago. Even after the railway line to Aswan was completed in the early years of the twentieth century, much freight continued to be carried on Nile boats, and it is only since reasonable roads were completed throughout the country that transport by lorry has become common in Upper Egypt. The amount of river traffic has considerably diminished in the second half of this century, although boats remain the most convenient and cheapest form of transport for small cargoes, especially between villages. One of the abiding memories carried away from Egypt

6 *above* The hydro-electric power installation in the High Dam, which generates most of Egypt's electricity. In the background to the right is the monument commemorating the construction of the dam.

7 *below* A ferry boat crossing the Nile not far from Cairo, with a cruise boat in the background. Few bridges cross the Nile, and the provision of ferries has been an important local responsibility since antiquity.

8 A view of the Nile Valley, looking north from the cliffs of Beni Hasan. On the east bank, below the cliffs, is just a narrow band of cultivation; on the west bank the cultivation is several miles wide. A new island with 'water-meadows' has built up in the middle of the shallow river course.

by visitors is of the ungainly, but immensely picturesque, Nile sailing boat with elegant sails - repaired in fact to the point of destruction - catching the wind in its upstream journey, or perhaps without sail as it rides the sluggish current going north. The Egyptologist is reminded that in the hieroglyphic script, the word 'to travel south' (or upstream) is determined by a boat with full sail, while the word 'to travel north' (or downstream) has a boat with no sails. Wherever there is a village there is a ferry, and the ferry boat is powered by sails, oars and pole. It is, for the sophisticate from abroad, a strange sight to see the patient crowd of men and women and children, of donkeys and other animals, waiting for the ferry to come; it is even stranger to observe a ferry in mid-stream with a dog in the prow barking fiercely, and seemingly placid camels looking out over the river while they commute from bank to bank as regularly as the city-worker on the 7.45 train from Tunbridge Wells to Town. The camels probably have the better of this regular experience. The sight further invokes scenes in several Theban tomb-chapels of the New Kingdom in which transport boats are shown coming to land with animals on board, straining their heads forward in anticipation of the end of their journey.

The Nile boat, or felucca, sits low in the water, and when it is loaded fully it seems a very hazardous conveyance and likely to founder at the slightest disturbance of the river surface by a passing steamer or tug-boat with barges in tow. Again the sight of boats piled high with pots, or bales of cotton, or piles of sugar cane, perpetuates the idea of the river as the highway of Egypt. The skills of the boatmen are not to be underestimated. Anyone who has sailed round the islands at Aswan knows how well the apparently casual sailors handle their craft - so clumsy in construction they seem until they are in mid-stream, speeding before the wind, tacking back and forth, gliding gently to land. To sail at Aswan is not easy because the winds are very unpredictable; but at least there is a good depth of water there. Further north the sailing is more difficult because of the shallowness of the water and the presence of the mud-banks we have already noticed. This shallowness surprises visitors, who expect the Nile to be like the Mississippi. The dangers of travelling on the latter, so well recalled by Mark Twain, himself a river pilot for some years in his early career, are very different from those of the Nile. But no one who knows anything of navigation and the handling of boats disdains the skills of the Nile sailor, and especially the *reis*, the captain, who learns to read the river in its changing forms and moods from season to season.

The low levels of water in the river which are so frequent today greatly affect the use of the Nile as a highway, and tourists are vexed to find that many of the interesting ancient sites, particularly in Middle Egypt, cannot be visited through-out the best months of the year. Most particularly they miss seeing the evocative plain of El-Amarna occupied by the remains of the city of Akhenaten, and the fascinating tombs of the provincial nobles at Beni Hasan. Not only is the level of the Nile now kept purposely low to conserve water, but the construction of mod-ern tourist boats with screws for propulsion instead of the traditional paddle wheels requires a depth of water rarely available except in the hottest months of the year, coinciding with what used to be the season of the Nile flood. While it is right that water conservation keeps the river level artificially low, it is not true that things were greatly different before modern irrigation works interfered with the natural flow of the stream. Writing in the middle of the nineteenth century, E.W. Lane had this to say about working the river:

> The navigation of the Nile employs a great number of the natives of Egypt. The boatmen of the Nile are mostly strong, muscular men. They undergo severe labour in rowing, poling and towing; but are very cheerful; and often the most so when they are most occupied; for then they frequently amuse themselves by singing. In consequence of the continual changes which take place in the bed of the Nile, the most experienced pilot is liable frequently to run his vessel aground: on such an occurrence, it is often necessary for the crew to descend into the water, to shove off the boat with their backs and shoulders. On account of their being so liable to run aground, the boats of the Nile are generally made to draw rather more water at the head than at the stern; and hence the rudder is necessarily wide.

This practice can still be observed in the traditional Nile boat, always, apparently, very old and about to fall to pieces, even though new craft can often be seen under construction in the boatyards at Aswan and Luxor and at places in Middle Egypt like Girga and Akhmim. Tourist boats with heavy screws at the stern defy this simple rule, and it is no uncommon sight in travelling the river to find such a steamer driven fast on a mud-bank and threshing hard to release itself, like a beached whale.

Continuity in understanding the river lies far more with those who have to deal with the Nile at close quarters and for whom the study of the river in all its moods

9 The chapel-hall in the tomb of Khnumhotpe, nomarch of the Oryx Nome, at Beni Hasan (Twelfth Dynasty, c. 1950 BC). In the centre is the offering-niche; above it Khnumhotpe traps marsh birds; on either side he is shown fishing and fowling.

and in all weathers is paramount. These are the traditional pilots and captains of river craft, who preserve the traditions of working the river which go back to the days before modern man began to disturb the natural conditions of flow and flood. These traditions perpetuate the practices of many centuries, although one may suggest that even in very early times there already existed a knowledge of the river and of building boats for the river which has largely been lost in modern times. Who would now try to barge down river an obelisk or colossal statue weighing hundreds of tonnes? Who could now in the boatyards on the Nile build a boat as elegant as that provided for the lifetime and posthumous use of King Cheops, and buried for him beside his pyramid at Giza?

Of the natural conditions of flow and flood just mentioned, the one most evidently disturbed is that of the flood. Since time immemorial, and certainly throughout the historic years of the Pharaonic period and for the first nineteen hundred years of the Christian era, the Nile rose annually, flooding the land of Egypt, fructifying the soil with a new deposit of silt, washing away the destructive salts and other undesirable residues in the land, and leaving the country ready for two or three harvests before the inundation returned. The cycle of farming will be

considered later (Chapter 3), but here we need to pay a little attention to what used to happen in the past, and what are the consequences of a century of planned hydraulic tinkering with the Nile. From a topographical point of view the most noticeable change in the character of the riverine scene, observed best from the river when travelling upon it, is the erosion of the high banks built up from millennia of deposits of silt, and, as a consequence, the creation of islands in the river and what can only be described as water-meadows. Such were never seen before the 1970s when the effects of the first ten years of absence of annual flood began to take an inexorable toll on the channel of the river. The erosion, caused partly by the wash of faster and more powerful boats than ever cruised the river formerly, and partly through the lack of annual 'refreshment' by the flood, both diminishes the cultivated area of the land and leads to changes in the flow of the river. In a sense the new lands - the islands and the water-meadows - have brought something fresh to the Nile scene, unaccounted land for grazing in particular, usable for some cultivation and ideal as staging places for migratory birds.

In the days before the High Dam was built, and even more so before the Aswan Dam was placed across the flow of this greatest of rivers, the Nile, unbuttoned you

10 A model boat engaged in the symbolic pilgrimage to Abydos, an act of faith by which the deceased hoped to benefit from contact with Osiris, Lord of the West; on a bier lies his mummified body, mourned by women (Twelfth Dynasty, c. 1900 BC; British Museum, 9524).

might say, behaved as it wanted, flowed when and where it wanted, rose and fell as much as it wanted in its proper seasons. It was ever both the saviour and potentially the most destructive element in Egypt. As the annual inundation brought life to the land, its beginning was until recent years marked by a festival and ceremonies which are thought to be traceable back to Pharaonic times, even though such continuity cannot be documented. The festival started on the night of 18 June, a date fixed by the Coptic calendar which is not variable like the Islamic lunar year. This is the Leilat en-Nuqta, 'night of the drop', the drop being the tear of Isis according to ancient tradition, or a drop from heaven, to be more orthodox in description - a drop which falls into the Nile and causes it to rise. Many people used to spend the night on the banks of the river to observe, notionally, the phenomenon, and many houses put out pieces of dough, one for each member of the household; if the dough rose, it would be well for its owner in the coming year. Later, as the days passed toward the rising of the river, wardens or town-criers went about Cairo announcing the extent of the rise in level. Excitement culminated at the height of the inundation in the middle of August, when a dam separating the Nile from El-Khalig, the city canal, was breached. This moment provided the signal for the opening of the inundation canals throughout Egypt, and it was celebrated as a great festival with fireworks, ceremonies and all kinds of entertainments. Although the actual breaching of the dam ceased with the filling in of the Cairo canal in the late nineteenth century, the coincidental ceremonies still continue.

There is no way of confirming the antiquity of such an occasion, but it may be doubted whether in its recent form it goes back beyond medieval times. Festivals of this kind in Egypt, both ancient and medieval, tend to be based on place, and Cairo, with its precursor Fustat, is a relatively young settlement in Egyptian terms. No doubt, however, can be cast on the importance of the river in inundation in ancient times. The Nile as a river was appreciated for its practical advantages, but the Nile in inundation was the god Hapy, usually represented as an epicene figure (although considered as male) with large pendent breasts and with a clump of papyrus plants on his head, and often carrying the rich fruits of the lands. Hapy was the embodiment of fertility - agricultural fertility in particular - honoured in all the temples of the land.

It was the inundation that caused Egypt to be seen as the gift of the river, and the awe and respect devoted to the inundation throughout history were its proper due. So important was the flood seen to be that its levels were recorded at significant points throughout the land, by constructional devices now called Nilometers. The well-preserved and much visited example on the island of Elephantine at Aswan shows clearly the march of the levels from ancient times right up to the recent past. But all the recording in the world would not compensate for a low Nile, when the land would be parched, or for a high Nile, when the destructive forces of the water might be even more damaging to the land. Direct invocations of the gods, particularly the great sun-god Re and Hapy, the Nile in flood, were about as much as the ancients could do to ensure that there would be a good, but not excessive, superfluity of water when the inundation subsided in the autumn. What they could do was to make certain that the best would be made of the water that was granted by the beneficent deities. It is sure that by the time of the unification of Upper and Lower Egypt, at the beginning of the Dynastic Period, Egyptian rulers and administrators understood that by the sensible construction of canals, and by co-ordinating water resources throughout the land, much could be made of even very low Niles. Whenever central authority broke down, as it did periodically, especially in those anarchic times known as the First and Second Intermediate Periods, the danger of poor irrigation and inadequate distribution of harvested crops would always intensify the effects of low Niles. The good local official, the nomarch or feudal lord of a nome or province, would boast in his tomb inscription that he ensured that no one went hungry in his province when the floods failed. In times of good administration, the effective lines of control from north to south would normally be able to meet the problems of shortages and avoid consequential famine.

In Egypt the rising of the Nile and the flooding of the land were regular and expected, and no special steps could be taken to prevent the destruction caused by the very occasional high Nile. During the time of the flood the Nile assumed a character quite different from that of its relatively placid flow for eight months of the year. The body of water coming north from equatorial Africa and Ethiopia so greatly increased the stream that in places where the Nile was confined within high rocky banks, as at the great cataract at Aswan and at the quarry region of Gebel es-Silsila, about forty miles north of Aswan, the water rushed tumultuously along, providing a vivid impression of the divine forces that were contained in its turbid depths. The whole point of the inundation was that it should inundate, and its result was commonly the conversion of the whole of the cultivated area of Egypt into a shallow lake, criss-crossed by raised roads and paths and interrupted by the

slight eminences of villages and towns. Levées such as protect the basin of the Mississippi Delta from flooding would have done nothing for the Nile Delta. So, very high floods in Egypt would flood rather more land than usual, and there would be serious loss of buildings, roads, livestock, and even humans.

Since the building of the High Dam, things have changed dramatically. There is no longer an annual flood. People may still gather on the river banks on Leilat en-Nuqta to celebrate the prospective flood, and one may even contemplate a time in the future when the meaning of the event will be generally forgotten, or transmuted into some new tradition. The continuity will lie in the festivities and not in the once momentous annual occasion. The old miracle of the inundation will gain a new significance. When the floods ceased to arrive in the years following the completion of the High Dam, the Egyptian farmers were utterly perplexed. Of course they had been warned not to expect what they and their ancestors had expected since the time when the Nile Valley was first settled by cultivators. Life on the land was substantially changed, and water came to the canals by kind permission of the authorities. Early forebodings of the long-term effects of the lack of an annual inundation are still worrying those who are concerned about the land of Egypt and its vital water economy. But the Nile continues to run, to fructify the fields, to quench the thirst and, less obviously, to generate the electricity that sustains the industry of Egypt. The flow of the river remains the country's greatest donor, even if it now receives less in the way of annual contributions towards its welfare.

All these bothersome implications can easily evaporate if, in Middle Egypt, you cross from west to east in a ferry boat, maintained by the local community just as in antiquity the nomarch provided a ferry for his people. Time can slip away as the boat is rowed or poled across the stream. You could be a minor official of the Eighteenth Dynasty, crossing the river to check on work in the quarries or to disturb the rural peace with your tax-assessing equipment. The scene has hardly changed, and the river remains the dominant element.

11 The crocodile god Sobk offers life to King Amenophis III (Eighteenth Dynasty, c. 1365 BC): a remarkable double statue in Egyptian alabaster. It was found in a secret chamber in a canal at Dahamsha, south of Luxor, in a region specially sacred to this crocodile deity (Luxor Museum, J155).

The Desert: Place of Spirits

On the Coptic Orthodox Easter Monday there is a general holiday in Egypt, which again is most marked in the urban areas of Cairo and Lower Egypt. Although it is, like all events linked to Easter, a somewhat moveable feast, it does represent the coming of spring, and, to that extent, is at the right time of the year. In the words of the famous Baedeker Guide to Egypt, 'All shops are closed, and many families spend the day in the country'. It is indeed a time for picnics, and for many it used to mean a trip to the great Nile Barrage about twelve miles north of Cairo, where the network of waterways and waterworks and the splendid gardens offered a most agreeable place to greet the spring, to 'sniff the breeze of the west wind' - for so the festival was called, Shamm en-Nesim. In more recent years the vast increase in Cairo's population has made the Delta excursion less attractive, and many people take their picnics to the Giza plateau, in the shade of the pyramids, or drive to the Faiyum across the desert from Giza, the goal being the equally pleasant groves of that lush district. But, apart from a few rare souls, Egyptians do not drive into the desert in search of romance and solitude; for the desert is a place of spirits, usually not well-disposed towards visitors; there is no water, there are dangerous creatures, it is too hot by day, and at night too cold to be endured.

There are, of course, people who relish the desert, above all the tribes of bedouin who still pursue a precarious existence with goats and camels, moving among the rock *wadis* (valleys) of the Eastern Desert and the Sinai peninsula in particular. The Egyptians who live in towns and in rural communities, the farmers or *fellahin*, do

12 The Greek Orthodox monastery of St Catherine in the wilderness of Sinai. Gebel Musa, the Mountain of Moses, towers over the fortified enclosure. The monastery has been continuously occupied since it was founded in the 6th century.

13 The hall of the tomb-
chapel of Khety, nomarch
of the Oryx nome
at Beni Hasan in the late
Eleventh Dynasty
(c. 2050 BC). The wall
on the left carries
painted scenes of hunting
in the desert, and the
rear wall scenes of men
wrestling, a theme
unique to the Beni
Hasan tombs.

not readily leave the green of the cultivation except perhaps to sit on the edge of the desert plateau, but looking down into the valley and not over the vast expanse of sand and mountain.

It was always so, except for those early Christians who sought the loneliness of the desert and the terrors of that harsh environment to purge their souls of evil and approach that much closer to the Deity. We shall have another look at them shortly when we consider the monasteries of the Wadi Natrun. For most people, however, you might go up to the desert - for you always went up, just as you always descended to the valley - for a particular purpose; you did not take your constitutional stroll away from the cosy familiarity of the fields; you certainly did not go there in the evening or at night. The known and visible hazards, apart from the simple physical difficulties of rough terrain and dangerous temperatures, were lions and snakes and scorpions, and, strangely, gazelles; the last were feared perhaps because they were of the desert and moved so quickly, and were therefore inherently dangerous. There were also the spirits which could not be seen: the Western Desert, in its verges by the valley, was the proper place for burials; it was to the West that the dead invariably went. But why were the souls of the dead dangerous? Some people were known to have been bad in their lifetimes, and so would not have succeeded in making the passage to the Field of Reeds, the ancient Egyptian Elysian Fields, the realm of Osiris, King of the Underworld. So, there were multitudes of mean spirits about, especially in the desert, waiting to terrify and harm the unwary.

There were also all those creatures of the imagination, the physical presences that lay behind the shadows cast by flickering fire and torch, equally ready to pursue the unfortunate person who might be overtaken by night away from the Nile Valley. Pictorial representations of some of these creatures were included in the paintings in the tomb of the great lords, the nomarchs of the Oryx Nome, at Beni Hasan in Middle Egypt. Hunting scenes may be seen in four of the best tombs of Eleventh and Twelfth Dynasty date. The most exciting hunting was found in the desert, and, as was proper for a scene in a tomb, a wealth and wide variety of game are shown, from the humble hare and hedgehog to the graceful antelope, the fierce lion and the despised hyena. And there are others, not well known to the artists, painted from descriptions provided no doubt by observers who had just caught sight of them out of the corners of their eyes. Not every creature is wholly unknown, but the reality is often far removed from the depiction. There is an amusing monster, named clearly in the hieroglyphs as an elephant; it is stout-bodied, with legs

14 A crescent dune to the west of Kharga town, showing elaborate wind patterns in the sand.

15 The natural spring of Umarli by Siwa town in the Siwa Oasis, with palm-groves. The dates produced by the Siwan palms are famous for their luscious quality.

like an ox, and has a strange protuberance sticking up from its snout. This excrescence must be the trunk, misinterpreted by an artist who had never seen the beast. But what does one make of the creature with long tail and an extended neck ending in a small head? Is it a gross invocation of the giraffe? There is, not surprisingly, the animal associated with the inimical deity Seth, slayer of his brother Horus, inhabi- tant of the desert; with its poker-like tail, long snout and long, upright ears, it is sometimes thought to be an amalgam of other animals, but is more probably a fiction of terror. Worried imagination has invented the leopard-like creature with a winged human head emerging from its back; and a tradition, quite separate perhaps, has conjured up the animal with a body sporting wings and a falcon-like head, named *sefer* in Egyptian. Is this the local version of the biblical *seraph* (in plural *seraphim*) described by Isaiah as having six wings and usually thought of as being of human form? If you need to depict a *sefer* or a *seraph*, presumably your imagination is your guide.

You might, then, go hunting in the desert, bravely carrying bow and spear and accompanied by a small army of companions and beaters. Again, you might go there in search of the hidden wealth which could be mined and quarried from the inhospitable rocks. You would not go alone, but as part of a properly organised expedition, established with royal authority and invested with an importance which may today be absent from the industrial activities set up for oil exploration or the extraction of mineral fertilisers for the cultivated land, now denied the annual anointing by the beneficent Nile. Industrial exploitation of any country is now thought of in pejorative terms. The disasters with which we are all threatened as the results of the mindless use of natural resources and the careless neglect of sensible procedures to avoid pollution, waste and environmental desecration, seemed until the middle of the twentieth century to have passed Egypt by. The local unpleasantness caused by the sugar refineries in Middle and Upper Egypt was nothing to compare with the 'dark Satanic mills' of the North of England, of western Pennsylvania or the Ruhr. Sadly, Egypt too, of necessity, has become an industrial nation, and the smog of Cairo can compete on level terms with that of Los Angeles. In general, however, the exploitation of the desert regions of Egypt has never been associated with the disastrous plundering of the natural environment, as in other countries. Quarrying, for example, which leaves such dreadful scars in the countryside of Britain, is somehow absorbed into the arid ambience of the desert. When the great High Dam was being constructed, huge quantities of granite rock and sand were employed in the works. The scene at dusk, as one settled down on the post-boat of the Sudan Railways to travel from Shellal to Abu Simbel, passing through the area of dam construction, was like entering a medieval Hell. Slowly the coffer dam which would divert the flow of the Nile during the building of the main dam, advanced across the river from both east and west; while great dumper-trucks piled high with granite boulders backed to the edges of the monstrous screes, discharging their loads to tumble into the water. Harsh arc lights lit up the scene, the noise was terrific, the dust appalling. It seemed without question to be a violent raping of the region. Yet that region had always had a violent aspect. Here were no rolling hills or smooth sand dunes, but only a terrain broken up and littered with granite boulders, inhospitable and not very attractive. And so it is today.

16 A relief showing the picking of grapes in the tomb of Petosiris, high-priest of Thoth in Hermopolis, at Tuna el-Gebel. The theme is traditionally Egyptian; the style strongly influenced by Greek conventions (4th century BC).

A journey to visit the High Dam takes the visitor through a broad rocky waste; slowly over the years the worst of the constructional clutter has been removed, and even a few groves of trees and shrubs have been planted to soften the scene.

How would the same region have been in ancient times when the same granite was exploited? Both in the Aswan district and in the more remote parts of the Eastern Desert, where hard stones were extracted, the life of the ancient quarryman was hard and unrelenting. In a place like Mons Claudianus, where a particular kind of whitish granite was extracted in Roman times, the remains of the rough huts of the officials and workmen are still to be seen. Water had to be brought to such quarries from some distance away; there was no soft prospect of even a humble peasant's way of life; there was no shade from the sun and little to protect one from the cold. The work-force was made up as much of criminals as of other kinds of impressed labour, and little attention was given to the safety of the person or the integrity of the flesh. The crushed toe or finger might be just the prelude to a more severe fracture or even death; for such were the hazards as the great, roughly

shaped columns and sarcophagi were rolled and pulled over the graded, but far from smooth, paths leading from the workings to the bed of the main *wadi*. From there the long haul to the Nile Valley fifty miles to the west, or to the Red Sea coast at least as far way to the east, was relatively straightforward - just hard work and very slow. But nothing was extracted from these quarries in the Eastern Desert that could be compared with the great obelisks which may be considered among the greatest technological triumphs of the ancient Egyptian stoneworker. The unfinished example that lies, still attached to its mother bed of rock, just a mile or two south of Aswan, remains a dramatic testimony to convince the sceptic that the extraction of such vast pieces of granite was truly accomplished by primitive means three thousand years and more ago. That obelisk, which when completed would have been about 43 metres (141 ft) long and 3 metres (10 ft) thick at its lower end, and would have weighed well over 1,100 tonnes, was never finished because faults appeared along the shaft as it was being cut and shaped. The trench beside the obelisk conjures up disagreeable pictures of successive squads of pounders and grinders,

17 A strangely un-Egyptian landscape in the oasis of El-Dakhla: a field of onions in seed. Onions are one of the country's most successful agricultural exports, and were in antiquity part of the ordinary Egyptian's staple diet.

packed close one behind the other in unimaginable squalor, toiling away day and night to meet a deadline fixed by others who would have no conception of how the wretched labourers worked.

The Eastern Desert, mountainous and rocky, traced with deep valleys and craggy outcrops, was, after the Nile Valley, the most important source of natural products throughout ancient times. Quarrying for stone was a continuous activity, although certain quarries were exploited only periodically. For unknown reasons, stones came and went in popularity from time to time. Some were always required, especially the building stones, limestone and sandstone, both relatively easy to extract from quarries along the river's edge; granite was also in regular demand for architectural elements. Yellow quartzite, however, was very much a sculptural stone of the Middle Kingdom; a particular purple quartzite was the choice of sculptors in the Amarna Period; schist became the mode, again for sculpture, in the Late Period. All these and other stones were found in the Eastern Desert, and were quarried when their time of favour arrived. There was also gold in those hills, and more particularly in their extension to the south in Nubia. The mining of gold was an equally bruising activity, but so successfully was it pursued in antiquity that the optimistic hopes of modern miners have in almost all cases been disappointed. The ancient Egyptians were careful operators, and time and labour were less important to them than the tangible result. They may have left a little gold in the seams they worked, but such residues were, it would seem, not worth the trouble even for their painstaking procedures.

It has been suggested already that the desert, whether Eastern or Western, was no place to travel without planning, and certainly not on one's own. In the days when visitors to St Catherine's Monastery in Sinai went by car (not even by jeep or Land Rover) it was forbidden for a single car to travel alone. The jovial Pericles Nikolaou, who used to run occasional car caravans to St Catherine's from Suez by way of the oasis in the Wadi Feiran, never travelled except in a convoy of three or four vehicles; and it was quite a regular matter for serious breakdowns to occur. The desert of Sinai was not an ideal region for camping. Apart from the usual hazards of lack of water and extremes of temperature, there was the threat of the occasional violent thunderstorm, unexpected, tumultuous, and merciless in its effect. Such storms occur both in the mountainous Sinai and in the Eastern Desert. The floods they engender, unabsorbed by the stony ground, have formed the landscape into a network of dry waterways, gullies and *wadis*, all just waiting to become

18 The evocative ruins of the Graeco-Roman town of Karanis (Kom Aushim), on the north-eastern rim of the Faiyum, a thriving centre of Greek culture up to the early Christian era.

the conduits for boiling torrents. A graphic account of such a storm in the Western Desert was written by Howard Carter, the discoverer of Tutankhamun's tomb, to his mother in October 1918:

> We have had an excitement which I will endeavour to picture to you. It seems, in this ever dry parched and scorched spot as if it has become the fashion to rain each autumn; for after time immemorial of everlasting drought, for three consecutive Octobers we have had heavy downpours, and this time a peculiar phenomenon occurred. While we as dry as a bone [in Thebes] the large valleys suddenly became seething rivers: Late in the afternoon, towards sunset, a terrific raging storm in the northwest was evident. Far away, at the back of the hills, incessant lightening was visible among ominous clouds, which at dusk became a continual blaze of light; but so far away that only faint rumblings of distant thunder were to be heard. Then gradually, the rush of waters could be detected - this grew to a roar - when suddenly, before one could realize its true meaning, a sort of tidal-waves of water came rushing down the desert valleys. The valley of the Tombs of the Kings, joined by the Great Western valley, in a few moments became little short of mountain rivers - the seething waters, reaching from side to side, taking everything before them - the torrent cutting out wide furrows in the valley bed and rolling before it stones some two feet in diameter.... And, what astonished the natives most was that not a drop of water had fallen.

He then describes the formation of huge lakes and the destruction of crops, and the arrival in time of their own local storm - rather less violent. He ends his description:

> I am thanking my stars that the great storm broke far away at the back of the hills, and that it did not break overhead, for had such a deluge, as it must have been, it would for us have been even more disastrous - I believe every house washed away....

Downpours of this kind have always occurred from time to time, but often at intervals of many years. In antiquity they were expected as periodic happenings, and led to the inclusion in the design of the great rock-cut tombs in the desert Valley of the Kings at Thebes of deep protective wells, or sumps, not far within

19 Looking out over Siwa town at dusk from Gebel el-Mota. Its remote position in the desert far west of the Nile Delta, and the Berber element in its population, make Siwa quite distinct from the rest of Egypt.

the entrances to the tombs. Such could receive the waters which might penetrate a tomb in a heavy storm; but over the centuries, indeed millennia, would in some cases become progressively choked with the rubble brought by the rainwater.

In a desert tempest it might be difficult for a traveller to survive unless he could climb up to a point unthreatened by flood. If he were to survive, there might be bonuses of full wells, rock pools, even unexpected and tenacious vegetation and carpets of flowers. But he should always be on his guard against fatigue and an isolation which might lead to disaster. Arthur Weigall, an Egyptologist who explored much of the Eastern Desert before the First World War, wrote lightly of the difficulties but graphically of the possibilities of danger. Describing the austere conditions on one of his journeys, he adds: 'A vulture circling overhead watched our party anxiously, in the vain hope that somebody would drop dead, but on seeing us mount again to continue the journey, it sailed away disgustedly over the windy hill-top.'

While the Eastern Desert, mountainous and inhospitable, is not quite what most people think of as desert - a rolling sea of sand-dunes with distant trails of bobbing camels and shimmering mirages - it has always been seen as a place from which useful practical products come. The Western, or Libyan, Desert is very different. It fulfils the popular view of a desert, although it is not everywhere the sea of dunes which is the true Sahara of Libya, stretching for ever, as it seems, to the limitless horizon. In human expectations also, the Western Desert is very different, and was so in ancient times. It has never been a welcoming land, and it has suffered from the promise of the same terrors of the wasteland already outlined above. To the west of the Nile Valley, once the desert plateau has been mounted - no great problem for much of Egypt's length - the terrain is relatively flat, gravelly in places, and folded in dunes elsewhere; it is not a difficult land to traverse if you stick to the established ways; and if you do traverse it, you will come to some very interesting places which have played important parts in the life and politics of Egypt over many millennia. A line of oases set in depressions in the desert provides welcome relief to the westward traveller, who today, it may be supposed, has in fact set out from the Nile Valley to visit them. In antiquity it would have been most likely that you travelled there as a political prisoner, or a wine merchant, or as a reluctant civil servant.

This line of oases, sweeping south and east from Baharíya in the north and on the latitude of El Minya in Middle Egypt, through Farafra and Dakhla, to Kharga

20 The ancient Coptic monastery of St Antony, deep in the Eastern Desert. Its origins go back to the 4th century, but this illustration shows a 20th-century church, and behind its left-hand tower a 10th-century watch-tower with 16th-century restorations.

on the level of Edfu, has always harboured outposts of valley civilisation and provided a system of protective settlements shielding the Nile Valley from incursions from further west. In ancient times their political significance was not seriously invoked until the late second millennium and later, when the western threat intensified and became actualised in the Twenty-Second, or Libyan, Dynasty. From very early times there were substantial villages, even small towns, inhabited by desert-dwellers who had more in common with the migrant tribes - now generally called bedouin - than with the native Egyptians of the valley. The content which these indigenous peoples found in the open environment of the desert made them more satisfactory inhabitants of the settlements which were gradually established in the fertile depressions. Egyptians sent there on official duty were uncomfortable in the remoteness of these islands in the wilderness; if their duties involved the guarding of prisoners, they surely considered themselves as much prisoners as their charges. To be away from home has never commended itself as a pleasing circumstance to Egyptians. This feeling of homesickness was often expressed in ancient Egyptian writings. 'Abroad is bloody' might well have been coined by an Egyptian. Even today, when travel and duties in other countries have given so many Egyptians the chance to see foreign parts, the thought of return is the great sustaining emotion. Often the wish is even more precise - to be back in Cairo specifically - a sentimental imperative that is confirmed in a sense by the very name Misr, which is used both for Egypt and for Cairo. A station-master in a provincial railway station - let us say at Kagug, a little halt on the line between Luxor and Aswan - will feel as isolated, and even as exiled, as anyone, convict or official, who has had to do time in the oases.

Someone with an open mind and a wish to experience something new will find the oases, especially El-Kharga and El-Dakhla, an unexpected delight. To begin with, their situations, although anticipated by reading and report, come as a great surprise. El-Kharga, which is likely to be the first point of call in any desert visitation, is so placed as to give maximum impact for the traveller who has come by car over the road from the Nile Valley - about 150 miles from the point just north of Asyut where the journey begins. The Kharga depression is not so much a shallow lengthy oval saucer in the desert as a dramatic, but broad, gully, the descent to which is spectacular. There is no cosy clump of palm trees with limpid pools to confirm the oasis image. There is, however, much water very close to the surface, which rises, bubbling up unexpectedly in places, allowing vegetation to grow, but

21 The elaborate brick-built façade of a tomb in the Christian cemetery of Bagawat in the oasis of El-Kharga. Bagawat is indeed a city of the dead, with a great variety of architecturally interesting tomb-chapels.

sparsely, at the perimeter of this large area (about 150 miles long from north to south, and 20 to 50 miles wide). Much effort has been expended in modern times to revive what was certainly a thriving region in antiquity. But encroachment by drifting sand, poor husbandry and some reduction in the water supply make El-Kharga, and the other oases, difficult to bring back profitably into the Egyptian economy. Yet the nature of the environment and the availability of water from artesian wells point with hope towards a kind of market-garden area, capable of producing good small-scale crops. The dates from the oases are famed for being among the best in Egypt. The vineyards of ancient times could probably be revived with profit, although grapes for wine-production would be less likely to commend themselves as a crop than table grapes. Apart from religious scruples, however, there is much a good wine-maker would have to overcome in the production of a palatable product of steady quality and acceptable keeping properties.

Of the two dozen or so docketed wine jars found in the tomb of Tutankhamun, only one bears indications to suggest that the wine inside came from the 'southern oasis', a term used to include both El-Kharga and El-Dakhla. There are suggestions in ancient texts that wine from the 'southern oasis' was especially prized. Could the one jar put down for Tutankhamun's posthumous drinking represent all that was left of a consignment of Oasis Supérieur, for it is dated to Year 10, the last of his short reign; or could it be one reserved for a special occasion in the after-life? One gets no hint from ancient texts that old wine was preferred over young wine, or that vintages of particular years were specially remembered. With jars made of a slightly porous fabric and sealed with pottery saucers and mud stoppers, it cannot be supposed that much in the way of staying-power was expected, or, in consequence, even thought to be necessary. Nevertheless, the Egyptians did take the trouble to mark their wine-jars with the source of the wine (the château or domaine), the name of the wine-maker (the vigneron), and the year of production (the vintage). Why bother, if production was expected to be drunk fairly promptly?

The success of life in the oases depends to a very great extent on the size of the local population and its commitment to making a real effort. Much more could be done in this respect. Tourism has unexpectedly developed beyond expectation in the last two decades, and the archaeological interest of El-Kharga and El-Dakhla has been enhanced by the excavations carried out by Canadian and French archaeologists. It is now clearly appreciated by scholars and by visitors how much more went on in the oases from the time of the Old Kingdom than had ever previously been envisaged. Considerable temple buildings, cemeteries with tombs incorporating quite imposing superstructures, remains of settlements, monastic structures of the early Christian period, demonstrate a level of activity that has not been matched to any extent until quite recent times. Now the larger towns are meeting the demands of the late twentieth century with municipal developments, industrial structures and tourist hotels - the shrines of modern-day living. A part, perhaps a significant part, of Egypt's future may lie in the nurturing of areas like the oases, although more than the romantic attraction of living in relative isolation may be needed to convince enough people to make the westward trek.

Apart from the distant line of oases overseeing Egypt's western flanks, there are other places in the Western Desert where continuous occupation since ancient times has developed and preserved ways of life distinctly different from what is common in the Nile Valley. One may think of the Faiyum as an oasis in a desert depression along the lines of El-Kharga, but the thought would be largely erroneous. More will be said about the Faiyum later in this book, but here it may just be pointed out that the prosperity of this interesting district has throughout history depended on the amount of effort successive administrations have been prepared to put into the management of the water-supply, brought from the Nile by the waterway known as the Bahr Yusuf, 'Joseph's River'. Prosperity is, on the other hand, scarcely a word to be used about the Wadi Natrun, a quite extraordinary area of salt flats lying just to the west of the Delta. Saline pools and miserable reed beds make up much of the terrain, with great deposits of natron - natural salts used anciently in the process of mummification and in modern times for the preparation of detergents. At one time it was not so inhospitable, and there is evidence, even literary evidence, that crops were grown there as in other desert oases. But by the early Christian period it was already a deserted district and very attractive to the armies of Coptic ascetics who fled to the desert for spiritual testing and bodily privation. The monasteries which survive today, and even flourish in the atmosphere of religious fundamentalism which affects both Muslims and Christians, are vivid reminders that Egypt was the first Christian country, that the idea of closed communities was developed there, and that the continuity of religious devotion can be experienced more acutely there than in almost any other place, except perhaps the Holy Land.

Of all the strange places in the Western Desert, none is so strange as the Siwa Oasis. It is so strange that it may not even be though of as a part of Egypt, lying as it does about four hundred miles to the west and south of Alexandria and not very far from the Libyan border. Its inhabitants are distinctive, speaking a form of Berber, with Arabic being their second language. The small Siwa towns, walled and built up with multiple-storied houses, are also quite different from anything found in the Nile Valley. It could be somewhere else altogether, tacked on to Egypt almost by mistake. But even here the evidence of ancient occupation is strongly visible. Here was the Ammonium, known to classical geographers, probably the very temple building begun in the reign of Amasis II of the Twenty-Sixth Dynasty (570-526 BC) and made famous by the visit of Alexander the Great in 332 BC. Alexander came to consult the oracle of Jupiter-Ammon, a visit overwhelmed by later legend as the place where he was first supposedly made aware of his own 'divinity' and the place to which he was guided by the hoopoe (which was rewarded for its service by receiving its characteristic crown headdress). Now, like the southern oases, Siwa is famous for its dates, for other horticultural products and, increasingly, for its antiquities. Its isolation is slowly being eroded, and its inhabitants probably do not object strongly to this disappearance of their ancient privacy.

There are many places in Egypt where the overpowering sense of antiquity, the consciousness of continuity - of things happening as they have happened since remote antiquity - the appreciation that no ordinary person can make the slightest impression on what is so well established, are strongly felt. It is easy to invoke the past in a temple or a tomb; but in such places one must confess to the exercise of imagination buttressed by knowledge and a spirit of romance. The strong feelings which sometimes suggest the presence of a deity - it need not be a specific god - can occur without warning in buildings or in open spaces; it is as if generation upon generation of believers have deposited the essence of their devotion in such depth and strength that something almost tangible awaits the receptive mind. Egypt is full of such places. But for true calm, and for feelings of rich contentment, move into the desert; wander up a *wadi*; climb the hills behind Deir el-Bahri; walk out towards the monastery of St Simeon, west of Aswan. The strong pull the desert has exerted on so many travellers, and which so clearly binds it to the true desert-dweller, can be experienced, if only vicariously, through the quiet contemplation of the ragged mountains or the rolling expanses sweeping to the distant horizon. It can be a thrilling experience, as well as comforting; even if, for most people, it can be enjoyed in the knowledge that night will not be spent there. And, for goodness' sake, do not spend the night there - remember the winged *sefer*, with falcon-head - especially if the lightning flashes, the thunder roars and it begins to rain.

22 The temple of Agurmi in Siwa Oasis, identified as the shrine containing the oracle of Jupiter Ammon where Alexander the Great is said to have discovered his divinity.

23 *overleaf* The great 7th-century fortified monastery of St Simeon in the desert west of Aswan. Although abandoned as a monastic institution in the 13th century, it is still used today for religious services on special occasions.

Procession of the Harvests

The late twentieth century may not be the best time to write about the timeless quality of the Egyptian countryside, to expand on the continuities of practices which seem to have been handed down, from generation to generation, since time immemorial. The present period is one of immense change in all aspects of Egyptian life, and there have been developments in the last quarter of a century that have led to fundamental, even revolutionary, shifts in the ways of agriculture and the organisation of the land.

The impetus for change did come, as seems proper in retrospect, from the revolution of 1952 which transformed the arrangements of life on the land. Up until that time, the greatest part of the cultivated land of Egypt was owned by wealthy families, some of whom were traditional landowners and ran their estates in ways formalised, if not atrophied, over centuries of possession. The characteristic regime was not particularly benevolent, although there were many exceptional families who took pride in the management of their land and in their care for the peasants who worked for them. Many schools and hospitals in the countryside, especially in the Delta, were founded privately, and children who grew up on the accompanying estates had the opportunity for some advancement out of the poverty and ignorance which formed the lot of most Egyptian *fellahin*. Indeed, it was from among the numbers of such slightly privileged young people that came, ironically, many of those who were to organise the revolution when it happened.

One of the main national reforms which followed what was a remarkably unviolent

24 Mohamed Ali Amer, a farmer, stands in his field of maize a few miles west of Siwa town. An abundance of springs makes this small region a true oasis in the barren Western Desert, and a flourishing market-garden area.

revolution involved the confiscation of large estates, the limitation of personal land-holdings and the distribution of small plots to the peasant farmers who had worked the land for others since the dawn of time. The consequences of the break-up of large well-run estates on the one hand, and the placing of responsibility for the many-sided activities on the land into the hands of inexperienced, rather timid, peasants, on the other, were to some extent mitigated by the setting up of co-operatives and local agencies. They could help with the multifarious problems of seasonal agriculture and marketing, which had never previously been faced by most of the new farmers. But the trauma of being on one's own, being responsible for organising one's time, planning ahead and dealing with the local network of ex-ploiters, was very real and hard to manage. Happily, the persistence of traditional farming methods in most of Egypt, the absence of farm machinery and the regularity of the climate in the advance of the seasons through the year, meant that a man with the will to meet the new and testing conditions could secure a fair measure of success, even if he had no capital backing. Nevertheless, the years following the revolution were ones of considerable difficulty for many new farmers; and the effect on the large estates which had produced the bulk of the sugar-cane and cotton was close to disastrous. Those who profited were the farmers with large families who could make the most of their land, raising crops throughout the year and specialising in those products for which there was a regular, and even expanding, demand - the fruits and vegetables which traditionally flourished in Egypt's fertile soil.

To someone who visited Egypt both before the revolution and during the years following, there was little in the general aspect of the land which indicated the profound changes that had taken place. It was certainly not evident that an un-paralleled prosperity had replaced the former poverty of the peasant, who had worked on the land for as little as five piastres a day (a British shilling at the time). The simple methods of husbandry, the long-established techniques of irrigating the land, the primitive use of pack-animals, the donkey and the camel in particular, suggested business as usual. But even such a maintaining of normality was to receive another serious disturbance in the late 1960s with the building of the High Dam and the abrupt loss of the annual inundation. It is hard for people who live in countries that have variable, unpredictable climates to comprehend the reliance that the inhabitants of some parts of the world place on regular and natural phenomena like the monsoon or other forms of seasonal rainfall. When they fail, the crops fail, and famine may follow. In Egypt it is not the annual rains that bring prosperity to

25 *above* Men shown winnowing grain in the tomb of the scribe Nakhte in the Theban Necropolis (Eighteenth Dynasty, c. 1400 BC). The grain is thrown into the air with winnowing scoops of a kind still used in parts of Egypt.

26 *below* Cultivation keeps the desert at bay on Dina farm, a new, privately run enterprise and part of a land-reclamation scheme near the Wadi Natrun, west of the Delta.

the land, but, as we have already seen, the Nile. For most of the year the Nile serves Egypt adequately, if not abundantly, and there used to be the annual flood. The ending of the flood was like the turning off of a great tap, an event which seemed utterly disastrous to the simple farmer who had lived his whole life and managed the fields in the expectation of the inundation. No amount of official information can prepare one for the shock of losing what has always happened. How do you meet such an eventuality, which may be unbelievable in practice as well as incomprehensible in purpose? How do you deal with your land, which formerly was washed free of noxious salts, liberally soaked, and anointed with another layer of fertile mud? The complex of problems, all to be faced at the same time, amounted surely to more than any reasonable farmer should ever be expected to face.

That the Egyptian farmer has met the challenges presented by the building of the High Dam, has adapted to an agricultural cycle that added a completely new growing period and crop to his year, has learned, if only imperfectly, how to use fertilisers to balance the absence of the annual deposits of silt, is a remarkable achievement for one whose life had scarcely changed since remote antiquity. Without considering the fundamental effects on the land of Egypt that have followed the building of the High Dam, the success of the Egyptian farmer has to be applauded; the continued profitability of Egypt's agriculture owes a huge debt to the traditional skills and the ability to adapt which have characterised the behaviour of the *fellahin* in recent decades.

There is one unexpected development which could scarcely have been envisaged by the planners, and which may have - may indeed already have had - profound effects on the life of rural Egypt. It is the advent of television. I have been told, but am unable to confirm the fact, that the whole pattern of night-life in the countryside has been transformed by the availability of the silver screen. In the 'old days' - those that might be held up by the sentimentalists as being the days of innocence and rural bliss - life in the countryside more or less faded away each evening with the return of the family and domestic animals from the fields, the evening meal, and bed. For some there might be the possibility of an hour or two in the rather basic coffee-house in the village or nearby town; for others there might be the occasional night-time jollification or *fantasiya*, when there would be singing and dancing, and story-telling. But for most people, for the greater part of the year, it would be an early bedtime and an early rising the next day. A village would be

27 Farmer Bayoumi Ibrahim standing in front of a huge, mud-built pigeon-cote at Tamia in the Faiyum. Pigeons are kept more for their droppings (fertiliser) than for their flesh.

28 Life in the Field of Reeds,
shown in the tomb-chapel of
Sennedjem, servant in
the Place of Truth, an
inhabitant of the workmen's
village at Deir el-Medina in
the Theban Necropolis
(Nineteenth Dynasty, c. 1200 BC).
Sennedjem and his wife
plough and reap in the
idealised after-life.

asleep by about nine o'clock at night, and awake again by five o'clock in the morning. The timetable was not fixed, but it happened that way because of the practicalities of life.

The advent of electricity, available for almost everyone at a give-away price following the massive production of power by the generators of the High Dam, was already having an effect by the 1970s. Even the smallest village was on the grid. Where once a flight over Egypt at night revealed only occasional pin-points of light away from the towns, now the panorama of the country spread out below - and this is very noticeable in the Delta - is punctuated by clusters of lights which signal the villages. With ubiquitous electricity, you can extend the hours of the day far beyond what used to be customary. Yet the possibility of sitting around in the dim glow of a forty-watt bulb, gossiping and quarrelling, listening perhaps to the wireless, was nothing compared with the compulsion of the television. How the ordinary family can afford a television set seems beyond belief, until one realises that such a precious possession - like a refrigerator or a washing-machine - probably represents the proud result of a year or two spent abroad by one member of the family, in Saudi Arabia, or Bahrain, or, until recently, Kuwait. To linger awhile in Cairo Airport will show the proud and somehow pathetic return from abroad of the migrant worker, his earnings, unimaginably high compared with what he might obtain at home, converted into the products of the consumer society. And in the village, the television set in particular becomes the household shrine, around which the family sits, night after night, glued to whatever may come on. Late nights mean late starts next day, and such trimming of time in the dawn hours means inevitably shorter days on the land, and even a lessening of enthusiasm for the day ahead.

Among the magical images of Egypt which summon up sights and sounds traceable back over the centuries are the morning and evening processions to and from the fields, the silhouettes of life etched against the dawn and dusk skies. There is a sombre dignity in the family group setting out for the family fields, father trotting along on a donkey, women with jars on their heads, children fussing around the animals, a water-buffalo or two, a group of unruly goats, perhaps a camel, all off to spend the day away from the village. The sight is best observed from a distance with the rising sun behind the procession as it moves in stately order along the narrow track or canal bank. There is a natural *gravitas* in the way that the Egyptian countryman moves. His children can run about, for that is their natural manner; the women may bustle, for they are expected to get a move on; but men ought not

29 Homeward bound from market in
Medinet el-Faiyum, capital of the Faiyum.
A farmer pauses by waterwheels on the
Bahr Sinnuris, just north of the city.

to be seen hurrying. If they walk, they stride manfully and purposefully, but not energetically; if they mount their donkeys, they proceed at the rate of a modest jogging, sitting upright and dignified. The morning procession is particularly impressive and timeless; the evening procession a little more earnest, especially if the declining sun, confirmed by the Japanese wrist-watch, indicates the imminent start of a favourite programme. It is hard to believe that the idyll of rural life may have been modified by the programme-planner's schedule. One may regret, but should one condemn?

Morning and evening in the countryside are still accompanied by the most evocative smells of Egypt, ones which linger in the memory beyond the edges of vision - the dunked madeleines of a simple society. Above all there is the acrid smell of domestic fires, built of maize and durra stalks reinforced by pats of animal dung, diligently collected and patted into shape by the village children and dried on the roofs of houses. There is the stench of morning easement, human and animal, of which one seems to be more conscious in rural Egypt than anywhere else. There is not commonly the welcome aroma of coffee, for in the countryside the economy does not run to more than tea. In closer proximity to a house there may be the pungent smell of cheap incense mixed with the rich scent of beans cooking by the slow process which produces one of the best, if simple, dishes of the Egyptian peasant. You would be lucky to smell flowers, although the Egyptian garden will contain wonderfully perfumed shrubs which may scent the evening air; but you do not normally find gardens with shrubs in the characteristic village.

It is perhaps sentimental to imagine that the memory-enhancing amalgam of smells is one of the enduring legacies of the countryside of Egypt. Even so, such a thought may not be too fanciful. Rural smells persist, as anyone who has had a long and intermittent acquaintance with any country scene can testify. It does not have to be rural to be evocative. Think only of the *espresso* or the Gauloise, and, once upon a time, the garlic of the unwashed. The sounds are there too: the morning and evening calls to prayer (now recorded), the barking of village dogs defending their territories, the crackle of the cooking fires, the rapid exchange of greetings and complaints as the dawn and dusk relationships are resumed, the domestic animal noises. All these sounds, individual and intermittent, are laid upon and punctuate the general quiet of the countryside. *Les sons et les parfums tournent dans l'air du soir.*

There is a nice similarity to be traced between the twice-daily procession to and from the fields and the content of many rural and agricultural scenes depicted on the tomb walls of ancient Egypt. Forget for the moment the essential purpose of these scenes - the creation of the right environment in pictures for the posthumous benefit of the deceased tomb-owner - and view them as they are, the graphic representations of aspects of ancient Egyptian life, and sometimes only details of these aspects. View them also in terms of the conventions of ancient Egyptian graphic representation. Scenes are laid out in narrow horizontal panels, or registers, and the elements, the figures of people and creatures, are set out in a processional way, one following the other. Prize cattle are brought in parade before the noble official; strings of offering bearers and offerings proceed, one behind the other, to the presentation; activities on the land, ploughing, sowing, reaping, and transporting crops from field to granary, are all set out in linear form. What we observe, of course, is so shown because that is how the Egyptian artist was accustomed to depict things. It was not his intention to imply that the single-file, processional, method properly represented how people actually behaved. But processions are processions, and things and people follow one another, whether singly, two-by-two or in groups. To this extent, therefore, one may allow one's imagination to make the leap, the connection with the dawn and dusk processions of today. Naturally, some ancient artists went beyond the simple convention to show gaggles of geese and herds of cattle, the individuals pushing and jostling each other, as they are driven forward to be inspected by, say, Nebamun, a scribe and counter of grain in the reign of Amenophis III. So too, in modern Egypt, the urgent procession to town on market-day is quite another thing: black-robed ladies, sitting and gossiping on a flat donkey-cart, groups of men in dark blue Upper Egyptian *galabiyas* and white head-cloths, striding out with metal-shod sticks (*nabouts*) quite as much for use as for show and support, camels piled beyond belief with sugar cane or cattle fodder, carts of vegetables and fruit, cages of domestic fowl, an occasional private car or taxi stuffed with the local toffs, and many on their donkeys, which seem so frail but are so valiant.

Although the superficiality of such comparisons between the modern actuality and the ancient idealised representation cannot be denied, press the evidence a little more, get behind the generalities to the detail, and the overpowering sense of continuity from antiquity to the present day will come through strongly. It is true that to get the sharpest tingle of *déjà vu* requires a fair acquaintance with the agricultural scenes in the tombs, particularly those of the Old Kingdom at Saqqara; nevertheless, the receptive mind needs only a few hints to appreciate how a vignette of activity, come upon even by chance in the fields or on the outskirts of a village,

30 Returning home after a day in the fields: a canal-bank scene on the road south from Giza to Saqqara.

may summon up an ancient counterpart of extraordinary similarity. The most obvious parallels can be observed without chance. You do not have to drive far through the cultivation before seeing the timeless group of farmer ploughing with oxen. The likelihood is that he will be using a plough of such simple design that it could have strayed from an ancient farm. The share may be of iron, forged by the local blacksmith, but the pole and yoke could be paralleled directly from a tomb model of the early Middle Kingdom, four thousand years ago. The oxen of antiquity may even look in better shape and more efficient than the ponderous and clumsy water-buffalo, a relatively recent importation. But the farmer of today will handle his team with complete assurance, and will do so even if, as sometimes happens, one of the buffalo is replaced by a camel. Often in antiquity the plough had no metal share, for the land, especially after the inundation, did not require deep ploughing; a simple turning of the ground to receive the seed was quite sufficient; and often, in ancient times, the seed was trodden straight into the receptive earth by herds of sheep or goats driven after the sower.

The succession of ploughing, sowing, harvesting, the transport of the produce to the granary or store, and, in the case of grain, the threshing, winnowing, measuring and storing, are all commonly shown in tomb scenes. The different stages are set out in registers, each process following the one before as if in real life the sequence was continuous. Nothing indicates, for example, the passage of time between sowing and reaping, for in the tomb time was not a matter of serious consideration. In all the depictions of daily activities, whether on the land or in the workshops of temple and palace, events and processes occur, if you so want to observe them, simultaneously; only common sense and the understanding of how things happen enable the observer to interpret the sequences in order, injecting temporal indications where necessary. The tomb-owner, however, for whom the scenes were prepared, should have complete comprehension of what is going on; their animation occurs magically when the tomb-owner requires to animate them. What might then happen is implicit in the whole ethos of Egyptian funerary art. It may be thought, therefore, that the tomb-owner may also, if he so wishes, animate parts only of the scenes. The idea of such manipulation of the 'tapes' of activity recorded for his posthumous existence may appear fanciful; but it raises a possibility which is not absurd in the context of the ancient funerary beliefs. It would be wrong to press the visual evidence, bearing in mind the constraints of space imposed on the artists who laid out and executed the scenes. It has always been evident that what is shown

31 Abu el-Hasan Zaker, a farmer on business in Luxor market, protected against the midday sun by a typical woollen muffler.

represents only a selection of the many stages in agricultural activities. Again, and magically, the gaps could be filled by the tomb-owner who would be acquainted with what went on in earthly life.

If such a tomb-owner were by some time trick deposited in the neighbourhood of an Egyptian village of today, one which was sufficiently far away from the busy modern highway and where the activities on the land were not aided by modern equipment, he would find much to make him feel at home; especially if he could compress the progress of the agricultural year, as indeed he would surely be able to do if his presence were to be magically motivated. He would recognise the ploughing farmer; he would be puzzled by the way grain was harvested, for in antiquity it was the practice to cut only the tops of the barley stalks with the ripe grain, the straw being harvested carefully and separately later - although how much later is not clear, for the second stage is never shown in the tombs. He would be amazed by the little donkey carts used to convey the cut crop to the threshing floor, for the wheel was not generally used until the New Kingdom. The donkeys themselves would please him, although he might be surprised to see people riding them; it is hard to believe that men have not always ridden donkeys, but there are very few depictions from antiquity. He might worry about the camel, scarcely known in Egypt before the Roman Period; its bad temper, inaccessible height and general apparent ungainliness scarcely recommending it for common use. At the threshing floor he would again feel much at home. Here, over a circular beaten earth surface, the harvested grain is spread and threshed, either by driving cattle and goats round and round or by having a flat-bottomed sledge drawn round by oxen; then, when the straw has been forked away, just as in Menna's tomb 3,400 years ago, the threshed product is tossed into the air with winnowing scoops to separate the grain and the chaff.

Our visitor from the past would recognise immediately the simple water channels between plots and the little mud-dams by which the modern farmer still controls local irrigation; he would appreciate the network of small canals by which wider distribution of water is made. He would be delighted to find the useful *shaduf* - that device for raising water from level to level - still employed. He might be too ancient to recognise the clever Archimedes screw, portable and convenient and used very extensively until recent years for transferring water in liberal amounts from small canal to field. Its antiquity is not assured, although its name implies invention by the great Syracusan scientist of the third century BC. He would see that the land is

32 *above* A wall-painting, now in the Alexandria Museum, from a tomb in the Graeco-Roman necropolis of Wardian, a western suburb of Alexandria. Oxen turn a *saqiya*, a device still used today for raising water, consisting of a wheel with pots.

33 *below* Picking flowers to make dye used in the production of coloured fabrics, one of the many small agriculturally based industries carried on in the Faiyum.

69

still well cared for, but that some strange crops are being grown. The two great modern staples of sugar-cane and cotton were quite unknown in ancient times; there are also many fruits and vegetables which are relatively recent introductions but which now seem to be so characteristic of the land - the tomato, the orange and the banana, in particular. Where now does he see flax, that source of fine linen and linseed oil, the first of which dressed men and women in life and in death throughout antiquity? Someone might explain how cotton has taken over, prey though it is to so many hazards in its growing cycle. What would our visitor make of the great feeder canals and the deep drainage canals, and of the mechanical devices for controlling the water supply? If he were to ask 'How flows the Nile?' or 'Was it a high Nile last year?', he would be surprised at the answers. He might, however, be rather pleased to hear that the *corvée* to rehabilitate the land after the inundation was no longer summoned. He might also approve of the new land formed on the mud-flats of the Nile by the erosion of the high river banks and the fickle changings of the river's course. Here he could find good grazing and easy irrigation, and - what was always sought by the Egyptian in the heat of the day - cool places to rest and to contemplate.

For most people who visit Egypt only for a short period of time, seeing the land at one season of the year, a somewhat narrow idea of the country from an agricultural point of view may be formed. Egypt tends to be thought of in terms of the Nile Valley; it is apparently always a green land where the farmer works in endless sequence, planting, tending, weeding, harvesting, and planting again. Matters are never quite as simple as they may seem, although there is a fair degree of truth in the general view of rural Egypt as seen with alien eyes. But it is a mistake to think of Egypt only in Nile Valley terms. People forget, if they ever knew, that the greatest part of the cultivated area of the land lies in the Delta, practically a *terra incognita* to most visitors and so too to the majority of archaeologists who study the antiquity of the land. Its ancient sites, which are many and of great antiquity and importance, have been poorly served by scholars. Yet it is known that this huge fan-shaped tract of country, very roughly a triangle with sides of about 120 miles in length, encompasses much of the best agricultural land of Egypt, land that has always been ideal for the creation of large estates and the growing of crops on broad stretches of territory. The written record surviving from antiquity is almost wholly concerned with Upper Egyptian districts and agriculture, and any picture of what went on in the Delta is meagre and unsatisfactory. New archaeological methods will in time substantially extend the understanding of what the Delta was like in the great periods of Egyptian history, and will almost surely lead to radical revisions of the accepted views about the area. It will be discovered, most probably, that the Delta was not a land of marshes and undeveloped tracts of scrub in much of the Pharaonic period. This idea, which probably persisted in ancient Egyptian minds as much as in those of modern students of antiquity, derived essentially from the stories and legends of the gods with Delta connections. Marshes, desolate areas uninhabited by man, pools and backwaters where the legendary exploits of Isis and Horus, of Seth and Osiris, took place, all form the ancient conception of the Delta, and derivatively the modern view of the Delta in antiquity.

For the reality of the political organisation of the Delta, of its cities and towns, of its active communities, there is, however, much evidence, often implicit rather than explicit. In the Delta were the great estates from which the king and his high officials, and the great temples of the land, derived their produce and their wealth. Here were the wide tracts of grazing land on which herds of fine cattle could be raised seasonally. So it seems, for example, from the account of the beginning of the confrontation at the end of the Second Intermediate Period between the Theban kingdom and the Hyksos, the Asiatic usurpers of the Delta. Apparently southern herds could still be sent for grazing in what was practically hostile territory at that difficult time. It would not have been done if it were not necessary and traditional. There were, no doubt, many marshy areas surviving in parts of the Delta, where hunting and fishing could be enjoyed, as was the case right up to modern times. Duck shooting in particular was common around Lake Burullus and Lake Mareotis, as readers of Lawrence Durrell's Alexandria novels will remember.

Wetlands, as all modern conservationists tell us, can be fragile areas, susceptible to draining and development. The Delta has been such an area throughout history, with periods of 'improvement' being succeeded by periods of neglect and reversion. For centuries after the end of the Roman-Byzantine Period, much of northern Egypt was neglected and reverted to a primitive, untended state. The cycle of change moved forward in the nineteenth century under the impetus of the policies of Mohammed Ali Pasha to 'modernise' Egypt. In the Delta lay the possibilities for expansion and exploitation, for the creation of big estates ideal for large-scale production of income-generating crops. The years of neglect which had lasted from medieval times had in a sense preserved the ancient pattern of Delta land usage; nineteenth-century exploitation, sadly in many respects, made such use of the land,

34 A herdsman leads forward a group of prize cattle: one of the characteristic scenes of cattle husbandry found in the tombs of the Old Kingdom. From the *mastaba*-chapel of Ptahhotpe at Saqqara (Fifth Dynasty, c. 2350 BC).

and pointed ways towards further expansion, that there followed a massive destruction of ancient city mounds. The destruction was all the more disastrous because in the Delta the ever-present existence of subsoil water, just a few metres below normal land levels, coupled with the general immersion of the land during the season of flood, resulted in the loss of much of the archaeological record. Additionally, the uncontrolled activity of the *sebbakhin*, the farmers and labourers who quarried the ancient mud-brick mounds for the matured ancient debris which so admirably served as a fertiliser, has led to the progressive diminishing of the old city *tells* during the last 150 years.

With the revival of the Delta in the nineteenth century came the reintroduction of the cultivation of the vine. In ancient times many of the best vineyards were in the Delta, especially on the eastern and western verges. The climate, through the proximity of the Mediterranean Sea, was softer and more moist than in Upper Egypt or in the oases, and the wines that were produced were evidently satisfactory to the ancient Egyptians. Things are not so good today. In spite of a considerable demand for wines for the tourist trade, there has been a notable decline in the quality of Egyptian wine in the last thirty years, and the decline will probably continue until the Government finds it possible and permissible to encourage wine

35 Children load up a donkey with cut sugar-cane in the fields near Medinet Habu in Western Thebes. The sugar crop is commonly gathered by camel and transported by light railway.

production. Marginal areas in the Delta, and also around the edges of the Faiyum, seem ripe for development in this respect, and ought through the application of advanced techniques of viticulture to result in a very reasonable product.

The Faiyum is another region where the cycle of development and neglect seems ready to be turned to reactivation. In antiquity this fertile region went through phases of great productivity and serious decline. The best documented attempts to exploit the Faiyum occurred in the Twelfth Dynasty (c. 1800 BC), and in the Roman Period. In the later time especially there was an extraordinary expansion of settlements and the encouragement of wide cultivation. Like the Delta, the Faiyum contributed massively in terms of grain production to the prosperity of Imperial Rome. The Graeco-Roman towns established around the verges of the Faiyum were models of successful exploitation in which a lively civic culture marched in parallel with agricultural prosperity. It could, one feels, happen again, as it could elsewhere, now that a stronger feeling for regional development exists in Egypt. The cycle needs to turn again, not just to maintain the progress of history and the pattern of renewal, with all the continuities implicit in the cycle, but also for the future prosperity of Egypt. Through the consideration of the past could come solutions for the future. Egypt is that sort of country.

Monuments of Eternity

One of the sights that punctuate the view of the river-bank as you travel up or down the Nile is the group of primitive brick kilns, often smoking and giving out an unpleasant greyish-black cloud, sometimes collapsed and pulled apart for the retrieval of the baked bricks. Near the kilns are the brickfields where the Nile mud is puddled and moulded into brick form with the use of simple open moulds. Side by side, in neat lines close together, the formed bricks sit drying out in the sun until they are ready to be piled up to form a new kiln for firing. The initial stages in production could be living demonstrations of the processes shown in a tomb like that of Rekhmire, Upper Egyptian vizier in the reign of Tuthmosis III (c. 1450 BC): the collecting of the mud - that most glutinous and adhesive material - its deposit in the puddling pits in which it is trodden and kneaded with water, a little chaff being added, to produce a plastic material just right for bricks. The slapping by hand of a proper quantity of the mixture into the wooden mould, which is smoothed off and left to dry, is just as it is today. Mud-brick production in Egypt is an industry of remote antiquity: the great superstructures of the *mastaba* tombs of the early dynasties were made of brick; so were the huge enclosures of fortresses and towns. The tradition persisted for thousands of years, and the late vast mud-brick fortifications of temple precincts, as at Karnak and Tanis, perpetuated the ancient practice. The very substantial Middle-Kingdom brick forts in Nubia, often recon-structed, again in mud-brick, in the New Kingdom, reinforce the idea that brick - unbaked, simple and economical in manufacture - was not just a second-grade

36 The west side of the Step Pyramid of King Zoser at Saqqara, the first great stone building constructed in Egypt. Almost 5,000 years old, it is a true monument of eternity (Third Dynasty, c. 2620 BC).

37 Gateway in the massive mud-brick city wall of Nekheb,
now Elkab, site of a great shrine and one of the
capitals of earliest Egypt. The wall is probably of Middle
Kingdom date (c. 1900 BC), but could be later.

building material, suitable only for domestic buildings. Brick - but not burnt or baked brick - had its place in the constructional repertoire; the modern extensive use of baked brick is one of those changes in traditional practice that is not necessarily an improvement.

'Change and decay' would form the essence of mud-brick building. Who wants a house that goes on and on, not easily replaced or modified? What king wants to occupy a palace built by his predecessor, or by an ancestor of many generations earlier? Burnt brick is rather final. It does not melt in a heavy rainstorm; it does not fall down through natural decay; it cannot be easily levelled and built upon; it is not in its decay a good fertiliser; it is by its durability a waste of good basic material, and not good for recycling. Unbaked mud-brick is a more versatile building component, and it perfectly suited the needs of the Egyptians for much of their construction, especially for houses and other domestic buildings; it was the natural organic resource of the country, producing dwellings that were cool in the heat of the day and well insulated against the cold of the night. So for millennia sun-dried mud-brick has been the stuff for the palaces of kings, the villas of the great and the hovels of the poor. Baked brick, although in principle known in antiquity through the accidental firing of buildings and by the baking of pottery made of Nile mud, was not extensively used until the Roman Period and was not even then adopted as a regular building medium. The fuss and bother of baking bricks did not compensate for the convenience of the unbaked 'primitive' variety; it is only relatively recently that baked brick has been more generally used.

Dating mud-brick buildings used to be one of the more tricky procedures in Egyptian archaeology. It is true that the basic product, the simple brick, has only in recent years been subjected to the kind of study more commonly applied to the 'respectable' and 'prestigious' products of antiquity. Sizes of brick and methods of bonding usually provide quite good criteria for dating, and are now commonly used by archaeologists as chronological indicators. But dating a brick building by using the old unscientific criterion of visual inspection could be very misleading. A roofless structure, partly collapsed or demolished, and subjected to the wear of wind, sand and occasional rain and the assaults of man and animals, soon takes on the appearance of an ancient building, even if it is only a few decades old. In the excavation of an ancient occupation site, the pattern of urban renewal by building successively on what may be levelled of earlier buildings is clearly manifested in the stratigraphy preserved in periodic layers - the precious guide to sequence used by good excavators. The various stages can be detected more easily in Upper Egypt than in the Delta, the essential determining factor between the two regions being the amount of rain that has fallen on a site on a regular basis. Where there has been little rain, as is common in Upper Egypt, the divisions between courses, and even between individual bricks, are easy to see and relatively simple to plan. In the Delta it needs the eye of a skilled practitioner to make out the same divisions; for rain will often have fused the divisions by melting surfaces and smoothing out sharp edges.

The processes of decay and renewal, and the consequent laying down of a stratification, can be seen in modern continuation in villages in both Upper Egypt and the Delta, particularly in those parts that are withdrawn from the river-bank and far from towns where modern industrial activities are busily practised. If you walk through such a village, where in all probability most domestic buildings are still built of unbaked mud-brick, it is easy to observe the places where old houses have been levelled and their areas prepared for rebuilding; it is clear also how the build-up of a village area has progressed over the generations, leading to the growth of a town or village mound (*tell*), the mark of an old inhabited site not only in Egypt but also in other Near-Eastern countries. Many modern Egyptian towns quite clearly occupy the areas of their ancient counterparts. It is perhaps most evident in a smallish provincial town like Esna in Upper Egypt, where it can be seen that the modern town level is raised fifteen metres or more above the pavement level of the Romano-Egyptian temple. An important ancient city like Sais in the Delta lies deep beneath the mound that carries the town of Sa el-Hagar. Such observations are scarcely surprising if only one considers the revelations of Roman London that emerge whenever a new building is constructed in the City. What is surprising is the amount of information that can be extracted from the careful excavation of a Roman site in London, and even more so from an Egyptian occupied mound, if only access for digging can be obtained. Objects may be few, treasure almost non-existent (unless there be a hidden hoard), but the harvest of evidence for earlier structures and ways of life, revealed through simple ground plans, traces of daily activities, fragments of domestic equipment, food waste, human waste, bones - a wide range of apparent trivia - is what rejoices the heart of the urban archaeologist, who even fears to find a treasure in case it distracts him from what he sees to be the real matter in hand.

There is much to be said for simple mud-brick - easy to make, cheap, simple to use in small or massive constructions, capable of modification and development; it

38 A corner of the pronaos of
the temple of Khnum at Esna.
The temple pavement level of
the 1st century AD is
substantially lower than that of
the modern town, seen in the
background.

is moreover a sympathetic material, perhaps not for grandiose (as opposed to massive) structures; it is an ideal domestic medium for kings and commoners. Kings, above everyone else, could have exploited the labouring force of the land to have great structures made for their occupation - flamboyant stone buildings, exploiting the noble tradition of structures in stone which go back at least to the Third Dynasty and the reign of Zoser (*c.* 2620 BC), when the first substantial monument constructed in stone was put up. But this did not happen. Such palaces that have survived, in sad destruction for the most part, reveal themselves as being very different from what one might have expected an Egyptian king to occupy. They were, nevertheless, provided with many suites of rooms for public functions, entertainment and for private living; gaily painted scenes usually incorporating natural elements - marsh thickets, birds, animals - decorated the plastered walls of the most important rooms. Some of the murals in the royal palaces at Akhetaten (El-Amarna) show a freedom of design and boldness of execution quite exceptional in the field of Egyptian painting generally, and secular painting particularly. It must be allowed that there is not a great surviving corpus of secular painting in which to accommodate the Amarna paintings, but they do compare most favourably with the fragmentary paintings that survived in the almost contemporary palace of King Amenophis III at Malqata in Western Thebes.

Furnished with splendidly designed and excellently made couches, beds, chairs, chests, alabaster and pottery lamps and vessels, known from actual examples found in tombs - deposited, as is quite evident in many cases, straight from domestic stock - and also from what is shown in tomb and temple reliefs and paintings, the palaces of kings and the villas of the great were by no means simple dwellings. But they were built for temporary accommodation; no king seems to have lived in an old palace. The evidence is not comprehensive and it would be a mistake to be categorical on this matter, but what is known about Egyptian kingship and of the exclusivity of the living king - the divine Horus - does indicate that each new manifestation of royalty was seen to be so special that the king's treatment in life should be as particular and as new as possible. For so the king would be treated in death, when he would leave his impermanent mud-brick palace for a tomb built of stone, truly a house for eternity. Stone meant for ever, and indeed, when one surveys the surviving buildings from ancient times in Egypt, it is no wonder that such buildings were though to be everlasting. The tomb for king or for commoner (from, of course, the right level of society) was required to be permanent. It was to house

39 Head of the great sculpture of the falcon-god Horus which stands in the first court of the temple of Edfu, dedicated to that deity (Ptolemaic Period, 3rd to 1st century BC).

the body, itself the residence of the individual's spiritual aspects which needed as much care and attention in death as the individual had himself enjoyed in life. The whole paraphernalia of ideas surrounding life and death, burial, the tomb and the afterlife, involved inconsistencies, contradictions, clichés and provisos, which, by one means or another, would ensure posthumous survival and the enjoyment of ultimate destiny. It was a belt-and-braces attitude, and happily it has resulted in ample survivals of physical evidence, among which are many examples of the 'house of eternity'. No Egyptian with ordinary comprehension of his fellow man, a slight acquaintance with the history of his own district and the ability to see with his own eyes, could have failed to appreciate the damage that could be done to the monuments of the past. Not only were tombs vulnerable to the attacks of robbers, and often, when violated, to re-use by others who could not afford noble new sepulchres of their own and did not mind invading the sacred privacy of the original occupiers; they might also be destroyed physically by men of later generations who were able to overcome any natural reluctance to violate the residence of a blessed soul, in order to make use of convenient building material.

While the kind of curse that supposedly protected the tomb of Tutankhamun and its contents against impious invasion cannot be substantiated from the textual evidence found in the tomb, there is plenty of other evidence to show that the ancient Egyptians regarded tomb violation as very serious. The tomb was its occupier's home for eternity, and ought to be respected as such; even as its principal occupant, the mummified body, ought to be nourished and maintained. There is not much proof that the care and protection of tombs were sustained for many generations, or even years, after burials were made, but there are many graffiti, visitors' scribbles, demonstrating that some of the great royal funerary monuments were kinds of tourist attractions many years after they were built, and did prompt enthusiastic comments. There is, it is true, a certain sameness about the comments. No doubt one visitor to the Step Pyramid of King Zoser read what an earlier visitor had written, and copied the laudatory remarks; just as people who write in visitors' books in parish churches or boarding houses are inclined to copy the comments of others. One may be inspired to comment, but what is then written turns out to be rather banal and commonplace. At least the existence of such scribbles indicates that the Zoser funerary monument, for example, remained in a condition worthy to be visited and admired thirteen hundred years and more after the great king's death. Modern excavation has brought to light the extraordinary series of small

40 *above* The pyramid complex of King Ammenemes III (Twelfth Dynasty, c. 1800 BC) at Hawara, on the edge of the Faiyum. The remains of a vast funerary temple, known in antiquity as the Labyrinth, occupy the area in front of the ruined (but huge) pyramid.

41 *below* A *mastaba* superstructure to the west of the pyramid of Chephren at Giza. The *mastaba* tombs of the nobles who served the kings of the Fourth Dynasty (c. 2550-2472 BC) were ranged in 'streets' beside the pyramids.

buildings occupying parts of the great pyramid enclosure, including those containing visitors' scribbles. The pyramid itself, stepped and not truly pyramidal, has always been visible, sitting high on the Saqqara desert plateau, and is a powerfully evocative image of ancient Egypt for most modern visitors. Go into the great court at full moon (if you are allowed); view it from a distance at daybreak, as the sun makes golden its broken limestone surfaces; drive along the main road below the plateau as the sun sets behind the monument in a blaze of technicoloured glory. It never fails to impress and to inspire, as it did ancient visitors like the two brothers, the scribes Hadnakht and Panakht, who wondered at the mighty monument in Year 47 of King Ramesses II (*c.* 1243 BC).

The casual graffiti of ancient times provide valuable clues as to how our ancient predecessors regarded the monuments they visited. Modern graffiti are not so well received. The European travellers who came to Egypt in the aftermath of the Napoleonic campaign were less respectful in their desecrations of tombs and temples. The deeply carved names of distinguished visitors who ostensibly admired the monuments are enduring marks of their lack of consideration for antiquity. Not even the great Champollion could resist the temptation to memorialise his visits to the great temples of Thebes, while Belzoni and Drovetti, the most successful of the early antiquities gatherers, seem to have claimed a large part of ancient Egypt's visible heritage with their names indelibly cut into sandstone and granite. One day in the future, perhaps, these testimonies of the great and famous will be as highly prized and protected as those ancient scribbled texts which tell of casual visits, of work carried out, of natural phenomena worthy of special mention, like downpours of rain in the hills, or of something as simple, but infinitely touching, as 'the sitting-place of the scribe Qenhikhopshef', written on the side of a natural rock niche beside the path between the Valley of the Kings and the workmen's village at Deir el-Medina. Here one may visualise that famous scribe with an execrable writing hand, resting for a while on his journeys to and fro from the royal tombs in the reign of Ramesses II.

More graffiti of much later date note the visits of Greek and Roman tourists to those same royal tombs at Thebes. Many of these great sepulchres, known in classical times as *syringes*, 'flutes', because of their tube-like structure, were already open and accessible to visitors, and some were even occupied by early Christian hermits, the like of whom we have met elsewhere. The occupation of ancient tombs as convenient dwellings is almost traditional in Egypt, and it continues at the present time as much as ever. The tombs in the Theban Necropolis may be the most conspicuous examples, but there are few ancient cemeteries in the whole country that have not been exploited domestically. In speaking of tombs, what we really mean are those parts of the tombs which were intended to be partly accessible even in ancient times - the chapels or offering rooms, quite separate (and often substantially removed) from the actual burial chambers. In the best private tombs in the Nile Valley, where the rocky cliffs were exploited, fine formal façades and entrances lead into spacious, well-proportioned chapels, airy and of even temperature. Such places were in a sense made for occupation, and the baleful influence of ancient representations on the walls could be nullified by a little judicious damage to carved and painted faces and hands and other elements likely to cause trouble. Throughout Egypt the destructive activities of post-classical Egyptians, Copts and Muslims are very evident in tombs and temples. In this damage can be seen a tenuous continuity from the practice observed in the burial chambers of some tombs, especially of the Old Kingdom, of severing from their bodies the heads of animals, birds and serpents in the hieroglyphic texts. These decapitations were deliberate and purposely included in the writing of the texts, the intention being to prevent these creatures from consuming the food offerings presented to the deceased tomb-owner. How could he rest comfortably in his house of eternity, enjoying his posthumous pleasures, if he were worried that the creatures in the very texts designed to ensure his nourishment might be grazing off his food offerings? How then could an early Christian family, no longer conscious of the niceties of ancient funerary practice, sleep easily at night in their tomb dwelling while the light of a lamp or the glow of a fire might illuminate and even animate the carvings on the wall?

Even today there are tomb chapels in the Theban Necropolis occupied by families, although not as many as in the early years of the twentieth century. Then a vigorous campaign was started to persuade the tomb-dwellers - usually by payment - to surrender their ancient habitations. They were not urged to move away from the tomb-honeycombed hillside of Qurna, but allowed to build houses near their old subterranean homes. From these new homes they could continue their ancient profession of systematic tomb exploration and robbery, sometimes even using a well-sited new house as the cover for clandestine excavation. Not long after the Second World War, a fine, well-designed modern village was built in the cultivation nearer the Nile, opposite Luxor, to rehouse the Qurnawis; but the authorities were never able to convince these wily people that they would profit from the move. The idea

42 *above* The entrance to the tomb-mosque of Qait Bey, the most impressive of the tombs of the Caliphs in the City of the Dead, Cairo (completed 1474). The door itself is carved with exquisite detail.

43 *opposite* The interior of the tomb-mosque of Qait Bey. Note especially the many and varied decorative elements and the outstanding calligraphic use of Quranic texts above the arches.

was good, the village was imaginative, and could have provided its new inhabitants with all the facilities they lacked on the slopes of the Theban Necropolis. But the situation of the village had its drawbacks: it was damp and might be flooded in high inundations; it was too far from the profitable hunting grounds of the tombs; it was not home, and few communities like being uprooted and resited. Also, in spite of other shortcomings, there is much to be said for living on a hillside in a tomb. Many archaeologists working in necropolis sites in Egypt have in the past found an empty, preferably undecorated, tomb chapel ideal for working and living purposes, and so much cheaper than having to set up camp or to build a mud-brick house, as is now almost always necessary. Flinders Petrie was a tomb-dweller at Giza when he first went to Egypt to survey the pyramids in 1880; Percy Newberry used empty tombs at Beni Hasan when he set about copying the scenes and inscriptions in the decorated tombs (Howard Carter, who was with him there briefly, commented on the excellence of the accommodation); Aylward Blackman did the same at Meir, where the decorations of the tombs of the Old and Middle Kingdoms occupied his time when he wasn't socialising with the big-wigs of the nearest villages.

In ancient times the service of care and protection of the tomb and its occupant was carried out by specially appointed officers who, in the case of private tombs, were usually members of the family. The exercise of what should have been a daily attention often necessitated the presence of the officer - the *ka* (soul)-servant - close to the tomb. He might live in or near the tomb's precinct if his own home was some distance away. Whatever the circumstances, he would be responsible for the smooth continuation of care, and his obligations might even be regulated by a kind of legal contract. As might be expected, for kings the arrangements were more elaborate, involving such established foundations as pyramid-cities and the complicated funerary cults of the New Kingdom, centred on the temples established for each successive king. Also, as might again be expected, the performance of the service on behalf of a private individual or a monarch would lapse in due course, through dereliction, natural desuetude, civil unrest, even positive political purpose. Nevertheless, in a sense the service could persist provided that the tomb and its representations continued to exercise the magical powers with which they were invested. To that extent the tomb was indeed a house of eternity. To read the name of a tomb-owner was a step towards ensuring his eternity, and it must be acknowledged that the rediscovery of how to read hieroglyphs has done wonders for the eternal expectations of very large numbers of ancient Egyptians. After nearly two

thousand years in suspension, they are once again, you might say, alive and well and prospering in their places in the West 'from which no man may return'.

The hospitality of the tomb, specific for the dead and incidentally extended to those who were devoted to the funerary cult, has a similar, although not precisely equivalent, parallel in the occupation of cemeteries in Islamic Egypt. The great burial grounds on the eastern side of Cairo, below the Moqattam Hills, provide an outstanding demonstration of how the necropolis, the city of the dead, can evolve into a city of the living while still retaining its principal necropolite aspect. Here the greatest monumental tombs, which are incorporated into mosques, are as grand, and architecturally as impressive, as anything of similar kind surviving from antiquity, with the possible exception of the pyramids. The remarkable mausoleums of the sultans Barquq and Qait Bey, of early and mid-fifteenth-century dates, still stand in relative isolation and can be visited and appreciated without too much distraction from the constructional chaos that affects most of the northern and southern cemeteries. For the most part, however, the old tombs are submerged in a confused, unplanned, maze of buildings, many of which are ramshackle and impermanent, others more carefully 'integrated' into tomb complexes. For the reasons why people live in such unusual surroundings are various, and their dwellings reflect this variety. Many are, like the ancient *ka*-servants, the people who look after the great foundations, the *madrasas* or collegiate mosque-tombs; their duties comprehend those of caretakers, of the equivalents of vergers of episcopal cathedrals, and of those holy men who provide instruction to the young and the faithful. They and their families dwell naturally and by right in the holy precincts. Others have set up their homes in and among the smaller, less well served tombs to escape the overcrowding of Cairo. There also are those who may visit the cemeteries on the occasion of the great Islamic feasts, and especially at the time of the *mulids* of particular Muslim saints whose tombs are located there.

Conditions in the great Cairene cemeteries are today very much more confused and irregular than used to be the case. Edward Lane describes what used to happen in the mid-nineteenth century at the time of the great Muslim festivals:

> …some or all of the members of most families, but chiefly the women, visit the tombs of their relatives…. The visitors or their servants, carry palm branches and sometimes sweet basil…to lay upon the tomb which they go to visit. The palm-branch is broken into several pieces and these, or the

leaves only are placed on the tomb.... They are also provided, according to their circumstances...with...bread, dates, or some other kind of food, to distribute to the poor who resort to the burial grounds on these days. Some-times tents are pitched for them: the tent surrounds the tomb which is the object of the visit...some of them (but these are not generally esteemed women of correct conduct), if they have a tent, pass the night in it...so too do the women of a family possessed of a private enclosed burial-ground, with a house within it; for there are many such enclosures and not a few with houses for the accommodation of the females, in the midst of the public cemeteries of Cairo. Intrigues are said to be not uncommon with the females who spend the night in the tents among the tombs.

The communal activities which take place in the Muslim cemeteries, represen-ting in some respects a kind of continuation of domestic association with the dead, are reflected in the behaviour of the Coptic community also, and may seem to be the modern form of what happened certainly in the Classical World at the turn to the Christian era, and in the more ancient Pharaonic times. There are clearly very different religious emphases between the practices of the successive periods, but for most people the fun and excitement of the festive occasions meant more than the religious implications. Respect for the dead in their houses of eternity is linked with a desire to involve them in the continuing pleasures of life.

Eternity and posthumous expectations are also very different in theological terms between those of the Muslim and Coptic communities of modern Egypt and those of antiquity, including the strictly Pharaonic and the classical of the Greeks and Romans. The last were never properly part of the Egyptian tradition, although much of more ancient Egypt rubbed off on the Greek settlers of the flourishing cities of Ptolemaic and Imperial Roman Egypt. Since the Islamic conquest in the seventh century, the focus of spiritual life in the country has been the mosque, which may also be a tomb, or incorporate a tomb, and a place for teaching. The mosque is, like any good religious building, a place of tradition and a place of expectation. It may subtly be more than most people might expect or even understand. The very first Egyptian mosque, built in Cairo in about AD 642, that of Amr Ibn el-As, the great general of the Caliph Omar, was formed roughly on the plan of an Arabian house with an open court surrounded by arcades; attached to it at one corner was Amr's own house. Undergoing many changes, enlargements, restorations

44 The mosque of Ibn
Tulun, the outstanding
9th-century religious
building in Cairo. The
design may be based on
Mesopotamian originals,
the unusual minaret with
exterior staircase being
perhaps inspired by the
ziggurat. The arcades
incorporate some capitals
taken from earlier
Byzantine buildings.

45 Chief guard Hussein
Mohamed Ibrahim in front
of the great temple of King
Sethos I at Abydos
(Nineteenth Dynasty,
c. 1300 BC), which he has
helped to protect for more
than thirty years.

(including one of comprehensive insensitivity in recent years), it bears today little resemblance to the original building; yet its immense reputation and concomitant veneration have survived all changes, and the incorporation of ancient building elements over the centuries, including stone columns from Roman imperial buildings, augments the ancient sanctity of the place. The tradition of veneration and honour remains strong in Islamic Egypt, and can be seen in the great mosque-tombs built in recent years for Gamal Abd el-Nasser and for Anwar Sadat. The modern mosques of Cairo continue the long tradition of religious building in Egypt, and in their exploitation of traditional crafts and skills are notably better than most other modern buildings in the country.

Many people who come to Egypt for the monuments of the country's Pharaonic past are surprised and delighted by the revelation provided by the Islamic monuments. The wondrous spaces of mosques - havens of tranquillity in the noisy city -

like that of Ibn Tulun (ninth century), the overpowering monumentality and gran-
deur of those like Sultan Hasan (fourteenth century), come unexpectedly to those
who are unprepared for one insufficiently publicised group of Egyptian
treasures. Not surprisingly, the ancient Coptic churches, discreetly moderating their
presence in a country of shared religious traditions of which one is more dominant
than the other, have to be sought out with greater diligence. Most impressive
is the church of Abu Sarga (St Sergius) in Old Cairo, almost submerged beneath
surrounding buildings, noble in its demonstration of an ancient faith practised for
many centuries under trying conditions; a building of great antiquity, built on a
place said to have harboured the Holy Family during its sojourn in Egypt.
As we shall notice in the next chapter, the visitor with a receptive mind and good
imagination will instinctively comprehend the sanctity of such a place, even though
in detail it may appear to be afflicted by neglect. The neglect is, of course, that of
a religious community that places greater emphasis on faith than on form. This
can be appreciated especially in the old churches of Cairo, but even in modern
Coptic churches there can be found the simplicity of ancient rites, often, one should
be warned, drawn out to inordinate length. The new Coptic cathedral of
St Mark in Cairo has already after only a few decades acquired an atmosphere
of intimate reverence which was never noticeable in the old Anglican
cathedral (now demolished) or in its recent replacement in Cairo's fashionable
suburb of Zamalek.

To return, if only briefly here, to the great temple buildings of ancient Egypt, to
Abydos, to Dendera, to Karnak and Luxor, to Edfu, to Abu Simbel, it needs a
different kind of comprehension to appreciate their religiosity. They were not places
of congregational worship, like the mosques and Coptic churches; but in their
time they possessed a sanctity and inspired a veneration which drew Egyptians to
them, if only at a distance. They too were dwellings of eternity, where deities had
their abodes, and as such they represented the permanence of belief and tradition
in a country where such qualities have been, and still are, greatly prized. There
are few lands where this sense of continuity is so manifested in buildings of all
periods. It is felt and talked about a lot in the United Kingdom, where pride in the
past may be stronger than spiritual devotion. But in Egypt, the length of the
tradition and the nature of its being rooted in the successive religions of the country put any comparable feelings elsewhere into the shade. In Egypt one may feel
that life and death are conceived and observed *sub specie aeternitatis.*

46 *overleaf* The great (left)
and small temples at Abu
Simbel in Nubia, at dusk.
Built partly to celebrate the
divinity of King Ramesses II
(Nineteenth Dynasty,
c. 1290-1224 BC), their
own survival was secured by
the skill of engineers when
the waters of Lake Nasser
threatened to engulf them.

Belief and Conviction

47 A young monk on
gate duty at the entrance to
the monastery of the
Syrians, Deir es-Surian,
one of the four surviving
Coptic monasteries in the
Wadi Natrun. Behind him
is an ancient waterwheel,
now discarded in
favour of electric pumps.

'A gentleman does not speak of his religion' might be the common response of
many people in Britain to someone questioning them about fundamental beliefs.
You may go to church on Sunday, but that is your affair, and the fact that you may
no longer dress up for service is a further indication both of a more relaxed attitude towards the formalities of life and of a wish not to appear to be awed by the
experience of divine worship. This attitude is by no means universal in Britain,
and it is far less so in much of the USA, where attendances at Sunday services are
strikingly larger than in Britain. Even so, Americans are not generally inclined to
take religion as a suitable subject for conversation at the dinner table. Grace may
be said, but that mostly will be that. It is therefore surprising for someone used to
the restrained - if not inhibited - attitude of their own domestic circles to the subject of belief, to find in Egypt a much more ready willingness to debate religious
issues, at all levels of society and whether the company is Muslim or Christian.
Religion enters into life with an immediacy that seems now to be uncommon in
many countries.

   Some people claim that as the Near East, in which vague geographical term Egypt
may be included, has been the cradle of three great religions - Judaism, Christianity
and Islam - there is something in the air you breathe, the ground you walk on, the
character of the indigenous peoples themselves, that exudes religiosity and encour-
ages men and women to think and talk in the terms of the great religious books.
As far as Egypt is concerned, there are many matters that have encouraged writers

and scholars to see continuities from the ancient past in subsequent religious developments. There is, for example, the question of the Virgin Mary, Mother of God. The idea of the sacred family was undoubtedly a common element in most of the regional cults of the country. At Aswan, the great god Khnum, a creator deity, had Anukis, goddess of the cataract district, as his wife; their daughter was Satis, worshipped particularly on the island of Siheil. At Luxor, Amon-Re, King of the Gods, was supported in a domestic triad of wide-ranging influence by his wife Mut, in essence the ultimate personification of the idea of 'mother', and their son Khons, a god of the moon. At Memphis, Ptah, the intellectual creator of mankind, maintained a family group with Sakhmet, the fierce lioness-headed deity, once almost the destroyer of men, and Nefertum, a son of mild aspect - in all, a very uneasy group. But the quintessential ancient divine family was that of Osiris, Isis and Horus, a triad of powerful influence through the very human nature of its many trials and sufferings. In the last five or six hundred years of native rule in the pre-Christian era, continuing into the times of domination by Assyrians, Persians, Macedonian Greeks and Romans, the images of these three deities were the most common of those offered up at the great shrines of the land. The museums of the modern world are crammed with bronze Osirises and group figures of Isis suckling Horus. These were the images that touched the ordinary Egyptian soul, and particularly in those centuries of political change and social turmoil.

The image of divine mother and child, potent in almost all cultures and especially so in Christianity, was already well established in Egypt long before the advent of Christianity, and its transition to the icon of Virgin and baby Jesus seems, from the perspective of two thousand years on, so obvious as to be certain. It would, of course, be wrong to suggest that the Egyptians of the first centuries AD deliberately engineered this transition; indeed, it is not at all probable that it happened in such a straightforward manner, or even that there was a transition at all. The most that may be said is that there was a powerful idea of divine mother nursing divine child in pre-Christian times, and that a similar idea was strongly rooted in the iconography of early Christianity.

There was, in any case, a direct Egyptian link with the Holy Family. It was to Egypt that Joseph and Mary fled with Jesus to escape the designs of Herod and the subsequent massacre of the innocents. The sojourn of the Family is an event accepted as historical by Christians and Muslims alike. Several places in and around Cairo are associated with their stay: in the neighbourhood of the Roman fort at

50 *below* Faience statuette of Isis nursing Horus the child (Harpocrates), the quintessential Egyptian image of divine motherhood (Twenty Sixth Dynasty, c. 600 BC; British Museum, 26298).

48 *opposite, above* Light penetrates the pronaos of the temple of the goddess Hathor at Dendera, illuminating the monumental columns with their Hathor-head capitals (2nd century BC to 1st century AD).

49 *opposite, below* The main burial chapel in the catacomb of Kom es-Shuqafa in Alexandria. A symbolic mummy on a bier is attended by Egyptian gods associated with death at this late period: Anubis, Thoth and Horus (Graeco-Roman Period, 1st to 2nd century AD).

Babylon in what is known as Old Cairo, there was a Jewish settlement where the Holy Family is said to have found refuge; at El-Matariya, near Heliopolis, on the way now to Cairo Airport, is the Virgin's tree, an ancient sycomore, under which Mary is supposed to have rested with Jesus on their way to Babylon. The tree - which is certainly a replacement of what may have been on the site in antiquity - is now protected by a small enclosure in a busy and populous suburb of Cairo. Its associated spring still runs free with rather better water than the area would lead one to expect; it is said to owe its origin and its purity to Jesus. At the beginning of the twentieth century, El-Matariya was a small, relatively isolated, village lying between Cairo and Heliopolis. Its divine associations were taken - as seems always to be the case in Egypt - as a natural part of the place, and the Virgin's tree was, and has remained, a respected local feature. A new and strong local association with Mary has developed in the second half of the century under very unusual circumstances. Unusual they may be in this case, which will shortly be outlined, but they are characteristic of that aspect in the constitution of the Egyptian soul which leads men and women, even obliges them, in times of crisis and strain, to turn to the deity in whatever form it may happen to be locally - pagan or Christian, Christian or Muslim.

At Zeitun, close by El-Matariya, is a small modern Coptic church dedicated to the Virgin. It was founded as an act of family piety, and it served a relatively small Coptic community within the largely Muslim population of this part of greater Cairo. One night in the fateful year 1967, the priest returned to his quarters next to the church after conducting a requiem mass in a rather more fashionable part of Cairo. He was tired and soon fell asleep. Before the night was far advanced, he was unexpectedly roused by a policeman with the news that there was a nun behaving strangely on the roof of his church. The priest at first dismissed the idea, for there were no nuns attached to the church; and what would a nun be doing on the roof at night? The policeman insisted on his getting up to see what was going on, and the priest was amazed to find an apparition of a woman, with a faint effulgence, perched on the small dome of the church and moving her arms in an apparently supplicatory manner. The priest could not explain what he saw, and could only interpret it as a sign of divine intervention and comfort by the Virgin to whom his church was dedicated.

No priest could fail to welcome such a divine visitation, and there was never any suggestion of sceptical caution on the part of the Zeitun cleric. In no time at all the news of the apparition spread round about to Christians and Muslims. There was no need to whip up interest; it sprang spontaneously from the natural curiosity of the local inhabitants. And very soon a suitable and convincing reason for the visitation was being voiced abroad. At that very moment Egypt was suffering from one of the greatest national calamities of its modern times, the Six-Day War, in which Israel inflicted a severe defeat on her neighbouring Arab countries, occupying areas that remain to this day disputed territories in Syria and Jordan, and also Gaza and Sinai (the last no longer occupied). It was an overpowering disaster, shattering the esteem of President Gamal Abd el-Nasser, ruining Egypt's armed forces and pointing to an even greater economic crisis than any so far experienced since the revolution in 1952. A blanket of total depression had settled on the people of Egypt. Some sign of hope was desperately needed. It was provided by the apparition of Zeitun, and every night crowds flocked to this Cairo suburb in the expectation of seeing the Virgin Mary with her comforting gestures. The phenomenon was observed and accepted by very many people; some saw nothing. Family parties could be divided by what was, or was not, visible. It did not matter whether you were Christian or Muslim, whether you were a true believer in either faith or a curious spectator; the experience of seeing was arbitrary and unpredictable. You could see it one night, but not on the next, when it was visible to others.

For weeks the visitations continued. Apart from the remarkable generation of piety and religious emotion, the nightly events encouraged an atmosphere of sacred enthusiasm and even euphoria, so that a kind of festive spirit was engendered. Booths were set up, food and drink provided; there were entertaining sideshows; a brisk business in the sale of religious pictures and images was carried on. Gradually the occurrences of sightings diminished, and as the country settled down to the uneasy aftermath of the war, the excitement waned, the crowds dispersed, the booths were dismantled. It has never been quite the same at Zeitun, but the church received an injection of fervour which has not been entirely lost; there are plans to construct a great new basilica nearby, where better-organised pilgrimages can be conducted. There are still from time to time appearances of the saintly mother, enough to keep the memory of the events of 1967 alive, and certainly sufficient to promote and maintain a new event in the sacred calendar of the country. It was all very particularly Egyptian in its inception, its development, and its acceptance as a seriously significant phenomenon.

The extent to which the fervour expressed in the early days of the Virgin's appearances may be maintained in the future depends to some extent on how limited the appeal may be to more than the Coptic Christian community. Many similar events are celebrated in Egypt, annual religious events linked with fairs, often lasting several days and combining secular jollity with sacred observance. There used to be a great many such festivals held in Cairo in particular up until fairly recently, but the vast increase in the size of the city, the mixing of neighbourhood populations and the dangers of crowd control in busy parts of the town have much affected the spontaneous fervour and fun which were, it seems, such memorable characteristics of these occasions. The most important Egyptian sacred fair, or *mulid*, to use the Arabic word, still takes place annually in Tanta, the largest city in the Delta, about eighty miles north of Cairo, in honour of Es-Sayed Ahmed El-Bedawi, a renowned Islamic saint of Moroccan origin, who lived in the thirteenth century and was buried at Tanta. The celebrations are centred on the mosque built to accommodate El-Bedawi's body, and they used to attract, it was said, more pilgrims from the Muslim world than Mecca itself. J.W. McPherson, writing at the beginning of the Second World War, describes the setting:

> The whole district [of the mosque] is decorated, and there are numerous public circumcision booths, and stalls for vending souvenirs and food, but no secular attractions, unless tattooing be so regarded. But if one follow the multitudes under the railway arch, to the outskirts of the town, one reaches the official and other tents, the place of fireworks, and a perfect city of booths, theatres and improvised dwellings, in which one can wander for hours, or so it seems to me, without reaching its limits. Yet its occupants overflow at night and sleep anywhere and everywhere in the street, and open spaces.

He later adds a colourful passage of description and comment: 'Several years ago, I think 1933 (1352), I witnessed a queer sight at dawn on the last day [of the *mulid*], from my window in the square, a sort of burlesque, but harmless at the time, called locally "zeffa el-Sharamit" . . . '. The activities McPherson goes on to describe on that occasion were quite marginal to the sacred nature of the *mulid*, but very characteristic of the behaviour of what would now be described, in festival terms, as the 'fringe'. Unlicensed, outrageous, perhaps deliberately challenging the sober celebrations of the *mulid*, this 'sideshow' provided a kind of safety valve for those people who, in most societies, exploit the chance of behaving unconventionally in public.

51 The complicated and elusive symbolism painted on the floor of the coffin of Djedhoriufankh, a priest of Amon-Re (Twenty-First Dynasty, c. 1000 BC), includes the dominant mummiform figure of King Amenophis I, as tutelary deity of the Theban Necropolis in late times (British Museum, 22900).

McPherson draws a comparison here with events which accompanied classical religious festivals, and his remarks put one immediately in mind of the great festival at Bubastis which is described by Herodotus in equally lurid terms. He puts it at the head of all Egyptian annual festivals in the late Pharaonic period. The goddess of Bubastis, the cat-deity Bastet, was identified with the Greek Artemis, and at the annual celebration people travelled from all over Egypt, mostly approaching the Delta city by river and canal. The pilgrims apparently came with little on their minds but the fun and entertainments accompanying the sacred ceremonies that lay at the heart of the occasion. Ribald actions and verbal abuse attended the passage of any pilgrim boat past a riparian settlement, vulgar gestures and rude shouting being aimed at the locals who lined the banks of river and canal, trading insult for insult and obscenity for obscenity. It used to be said that the travellers on boats passing majestically through the Suez Canal were subjected to considerable vulgarity by the shameless urchins who lurked along the way, eager to disconcert the gentle lady passengers taking their mid-morning *bouillon*. And so at Bubastis, when the pilgrims arrived, the feast was celebrated with great sacrifices, and more grape-wine was drunk in its course than in the whole of the rest of the year.

As far as the ancient Egyptian sources are concerned, much reading between the lines has to be practised to discover even hints of such behaviour as Herodotus describes. The fault lies in the nature of the surviving evidence, which mostly comes from official texts and specifically religious documents, the purpose of which is to celebrate the great cults in proper manner. It does not take a lot of imagination, however, to look beyond the scenes depicting ancient Egyptian festivals to detect more than the staid formalities of religious observance. The nature of Egyptian religion at the highest level - essentially royal - was exclusive and inaccessible to most of the population. Entry to temples was severely restricted; there could be no slipping in for a quick prayer or moment of contemplation, as would now be possible in mosque or church. If the deity was to be approached in daily life, then it could only be done by a kind of proxy act of worship, at the entrance to a temple or in a makeshift and tiny shrine set up in a place where a divine association might be detected. The workmen travelling over the hills from the Valley of the Kings to their village put together temporary shrines, sometimes with an offering inscription - personal and individual - where simple acts of devotion could be performed, in some respects like the calvaries found at crossroads and other convenient points in Catholic countries. The essence of any such place, in Egypt or in Europe, would seem to be the possibility of making a private sign of worship, discreetly and modestly, and informally. Otherwise, in ancient Egypt, the only formal opportunities for popular participation in the worship of the great deities occurred at the time of the festivals that involved processions and public appearances of the divine presences.

On the walls of the great Eighteenth-Dynasty colonnade in the temple of Luxor are wonderful representations of the processions and celebrations accompanying the Opet Festival, when Amon-Re, King of the Gods, travelled by land and river from the temple of Karnak, about two miles downstream, to Luxor to visit his consort Mut. The progress of the sacred boats carrying the divine images is accompanied by bands of priests, soldiers, offering-bearers, musicians, dancers. The trumpets blow, the drums throb, the cymbals clash, the crowds hasten to follow the procession, and imagination must supply the rest. More of the festive flavour can be extracted from an inscription in the temple of Edfu, south of Luxor, where one thousand years later on festival occasions the environs of the huge temple of Horus were alive with ceremony and pleasure-making: 'The priests and divine fathers are decked in fine linen, the royal company accoutred in its insignia, its young men are drunk, its people are happy, its young girls beautiful to behold, festivity is all around, celebration is in all its districts, no one sleeps till dawn.' And then, no doubt, everyone went home, somewhat the worse for wear but content at having participated in a splendid occasion, with even, if they were lucky, a glimpse of the god.

An extraordinary survival and example of apparent continuity occurs annually at Luxor. It is centred on the temple of Luxor itself, a notable example of ancient pagan worship for Christians and Muslims and yet a building that has for more than three thousand years been a religious focus in the town. After the decline of Pharaonic Egypt and the ancient forms of worship, part of the temple of Amon-Re was converted, possibly into a shrine for the Roman imperial cult and later into a Christian church (although this last transformation remains uncertain). The main body of the temple gradually became a thriving community of houses, stock-raising and small industry which lasted up to the mid-nineteenth century. The local British consul, Mustapha Agha, even built a house for himself high on the piled debris in the great colonnade, which later was occupied by Lady Duff Gordon. In late medieval times the mosque of the local holy man, Abu'l Haggag, was built intrusively into the eastern part of the first court of Ramesses II. It has always seemed fitting that a sacred building, even if of pagan origin, should persist in sacred use, whether the cathedral of Syracuse in the body of a fifth-century BC Greek temple, or the

52 *above* The colonnade of Horemheb seen from the court of Amenophis III in the temple of Luxor; in the background are the additions of Ramesses II, incorporating the mosque of Abu'l Haggag.

53 *below* A troupe of itinerant street musicians (*rababa*) celebrates the start of Ramadan, the Muslim month of fasting, in the *suq* (market) of Luxor.

54 *above* Bright lights illuminate the late 18th-century mosque of Abu el-Abbas el-Mursi in Alexandria during the month of Ramadan. As the site of the tomb of this Muslim saint, who died in 1288, it has become an important religious focus in the city.

55 *below* Children in Selwa village near Aswan. The wall decoration of the tented Ka'bah, Islam's most sacred shrine, and a man on a horse carrying a sunshade, indicates that the owner of the house has made the pilgrimage to Mecca.

church of Hagia Sophia in Constantinople, a mosque since AD 1453. And so the little Luxor mosque has survived, highly venerated locally and the focus of the annual festival of Abu'l Haggag, part of which consists of a procession in which the sacred boat of the Muslim saint is paraded through the streets of Luxor accompanied by the usual scenes of true devotion and general excitement.

How can one claim that such an unusual event, unprecedented among the *mulids* of Egypt, can be traced back to Pharaonic times? It could be said that the carved scenes in the Luxor temple may have inspired some of the activities, including the boat procession; but these scenes have only been visible in modern times since the mid-nineteenth century at the earliest, while the celebration in its present form goes back apparently much further. It is, however, no longer quite what it was. A description from 1925 gives some idea of what happened before rival attractions diluted the urgency of local festivities: 'Rather interesting survival of Barque of Amon. First gaily dressed camels and riders, most elaborately got up, then procession of donkeys, then sheikhs and banners, more camels with "howdahs"....then 2 boats on carts, the boats full of children. The "howdahs" - covered - had boys inside singing. Great crowds, drums, dust and heat.' So wrote Minnie Burton, wife of the remarkable photographer Harry Burton who worked with Howard Carter on Tutankhamun's tomb.

Egypt in the late twentieth century is undoubtedly a more consciously religious country than it has been for many years. It is evident in large and small matters: in attendance at prayers in mosques on Fridays; in the observance of Ramadan, the month of fasting; in the more careful attention to modest dress and behaviour by women; in the observance of dietary restrictions and the avoidance of alcohol by Muslim believers. The move towards stricter observance of the formal signs of good Muslim behaviour may in many cases mean little more than a desire to appear to be no less observant than one's fellow. Still, it would be an error to be too cynical in judging what may appear to be superficial piety. The growth of Islamic fundamentalism, generally and officially not welcomed in Egypt, especially if accompanied by political fanaticism and sectarian discrimination, affects all levels of society, and, by a kind of transferred religiosity, the Christian community also.

One of the most noticeable features of Coptic Christianity in recent decades has been the rehabilitation of the monasteries with considerable recruitment - if that is the right word to describe willing initiates - of monks, and the revival of the modest estates of these religious foundations. A visit after thirty years to the

56 A view into the monastery of St Catherine in Sinai. The monks have always maintained a good relationship with the bedouin tribesmen of the region, who bring firewood and perform other essential services. The minaret marks the mosque built within the enclosure.

57 The dramatically sited monastery of Deir es-Surian in the Wadi Natrun - an area of stark desolation favoured by the anchorites of the early Christian Period. It was refounded in the 9th century on the site of an earlier 6th-century monastery.

monastic communities in the Wadi Natrun, a little to the west of the Cairo to Alexandria desert road, revealed remarkable changes. The run-down, depleted communities of the early 1960s are now bustling with young monks, eager to explain the antiquity and unpretentious treasures among which they live and worship. Dorothea Russell, writing thirty years ago, remarked that these monasteries had not changed in 'aspect and essentials' for a thousand years. It is no longer so, and many who visit them casually today may regret the disappearance of the sacred decrepitude of the past, which seemed to be permeated with an ancient and enduring devotion. In a sense it seems inappropriate that piety should be practised in prosperous surroundings. Robert Curzon, however, who visited the Wadi Natrun monasteries in 1837 on the trail of ancient manuscripts, found both squalor and a general lack of piety. All the four foundations still active (at that time hardly the right word to use) were run down, scarcely manned with enough monks to keep

the services going. Yet he was mightily impressed by the setting for what was once a vast religious community of monasteries, cells and lone ascetics: '...although parched and drear in the extreme from their vastness and openness, there is something grand and sublime in the silence and loneliness of these burning plains.'

Here, as elsewhere in Egypt, particularly in the environs of Thebes, huge numbers of early Christians in the third, fourth and fifth centuries embraced a kind of communcal isolation. It would seem that their miserable cells were so close to each other that the desire for solitude engendered a particular sort of mean unneighbourliness. The neglect of the body and the nurturing of the soul made a strange asceticism which could perhaps only be practised *en masse* in a country where the days would be warm, even though the nights - in the desert - would be miserably cold. The need for mutual protection and the provision of services with priests led to monastic groupings and then buildings, and finally the evolution of codes of

58 Painting of Christ in Majesty in the small chapel of the church of St Antony in St Antony's Monastery in the Eastern Desert. The figure is enclosed in the sacred oval (mandorla), supported by angels, attended by the four beasts of the Apocalypse and flanked by the Virgin and St John (13th century).

111

59 *above* **Sheikh Mahmud, the Islamic leader of the New Valley, in the grounds of a mosque in Kharga town in the oasis of El-Kharga.**

60 *opposite* **A view from the walls of Saladin's Citadel, high above Cairo, looking over roofs towards the mosques of Sultan Hasan (on left, 14th century) and Er-Rifai (on right, turn of the present century) - the new harmonising with and dramatically offsetting the old.**

behaviour which may have made many a former hermit think longingly of his previously lone condition. It was bad enough controlling one's evil thoughts and mad fantasies (exacerbated by fasting and discomfort) by oneself in the wilderness; it was an even greater strain to keep them in check according to the rules and systems of someone like the great monastic codifier Shenouti, abbot of the White Monastery near Sohag in Middle Egypt during the fifth century. Observed day and night by one's colleagues, it was not easy for an inmate to backslide.

The desire to live under restraint may be a sign of weakness of spirit; but it should not be underestimated. It would be more charitable to see the ancient migration to the desert as a search for peace of mind in a setting free from other human associations. Something of the same feeling may be seen in the desire by King Akhenaten in the fourteenth century BC to flee from Thebes and establish a new city in an unsullied 'pure' place. In his wish to foster the worship of the Aten, the divine disk of the sun, in the company of his family and attended by trusted adherents, he needed to free the 'new religion' from association with the ancient gods of Thebes, in particular the triad of Amon-Re, Mut and Khons. The ancient deities pervaded the whole of Egypt; every place had its autochthonous divinity, and it was no easy matter to discover a virgin site. In Akhetaten, 'the Horizon of the Aten', he found his own refuge, and even today visitors to El-Amarna may soak in the special atmosphere of the place, notably potent if you can accept the vision of the deity in Akhenaten's interpretation.

Most people who feel the numinous qualities of a place can actualise their feelings in whatever form of god they wish to perceive. The top of almost any high, lonely place is susceptible of arousing pious feelings. For Akhenaten, it was not only the loneliness of the site of his new city that commended it to him; the very immaculate nature of the place, unsullied by human presence and without other divine associations, rendered it almost the only suitable site. Here he and his family would remain throughout their lives, tied down, as it were, by the purity of the great sun-bathed desert plain, surrounded by hills which cradled the sun at its first appearance every morning. Not many religious centres have been so precisely defined; but the ideas of purity and isolation remain potent stimuli for contemplation, whether in Egypt or elsewhere.

Few places were as remote or as striking in outlook as the eyrie on the Moqattam Hills, overlooking Cairo, occupied by the Baktashi Monastery of the dervishes, an unorthodox Shia Muslim sect which was peculiar to the Ottoman Empire and is

now in serious decline. This monastery, for so it must be called, was established possibly as early as the fourteenth century, and had a few points in common with the many Coptic monasteries in Egypt, in addition to the isolation of its position and the celibacy of its most devoted members. In organisation it had some similarities with the characteristic Christian monastery, having an abbot, or more properly Baba, and a body of initiates or monks. There used to be many different sects of dervishes in Egypt up to the late nineteenth century, and their behaviour, which for them was an expression of divine possession, made them a subject of great interest to European visitors. The trances induced by the repetition of words and phrases, and the extraordinary bodily privations endured with apparently no lasting harm, were impressive testimonies of faith and endurance, even if inexplicably misplaced in the eyes of those with different religious traditions.

The enduring of pain and the exercise of a kind of miserable athleticism by the devotees of religion were much admired by early Christians in Egypt, and the stories told about the early fathers of Coptic Christianity are full of unhealthy competitions over the privations of the flesh. How could you eat less than your next-door hermit? How few hours of sleep could you do with? How long could you stay in the sun, or in the cold, or in the presence of temptresses? The evil spirits of the desert, about which we talked earlier, were real enough to the tortured imaginations of the underfed, under-rested, bodily battered inhabitants of the desert hermitages. The fevered utterances of such people could be interpreted as being divine, and even of oracular quality. Similarly, what might be seen in sleep induced in a sacred place could also be regarded as conducive to oracular dreaming. This kind of dream incubation, well known also in the Greek world, was certainly practised in the late centuries of the Pharaonic period, and was probably not uncommon at earlier times. In a late account of a famine that supposedly took place in Egypt in the reign of King Zoser of the Third Dynasty, the king is said to have been visited in a dream by Khnum, god of the cataract region, who pointed the way to overcome the divine anger which had caused the famine. The importance of dreams is well exemplified in the Biblical story of Joseph. So too by the dream experienced by King Tuthmosis IV, when, as a young prince, he fell asleep by the Sphinx at Giza and was adjured by the god of the Sphinx to clear his monument of sand, in return for the promise of which he would be king of Egypt. A series of texts written in the demotic script on pottery flakes (ostraca) found not long ago at Saqqara shows that incubation, i.e. sleeping and dreaming under sacred conditions in temple precincts, could result in extraordinary revelations. These texts document in part the results of deliberate efforts by a scribe named Hor to obtain divine advice on matters relating to the operation of the ibis cult at Saqqara in the second century BC. Hor attended the so-called 'house of rest' of the Ibis, divine bird of Thoth, specifically seeking the god's intervention.

Edward Lane describes how in the early nineteenth century Egyptians might go to sleep seeking guidance from God in a dream: 'by causing them to see something white or green, or water, if the action which they contemplate be approved, or if they are to expect approaching good fortune, and if not, by causing them to see something black or red, or fire.' As they go to sleep they call on Allah to bless the Lord Mohammed.

It has often been pointed out that in everyday intercourse Egyptians of all classes, and whether Muslim or Christian, regularly include divine invocations in their conversation. Nothing for the future is mentioned without *inshallah*, 'as God pleases!'; the words *el-hamdu-l'illah*, 'Well, thank God!', are liberally interjected at every appropriate moment. Egypt is a country where religion fits easily into daily life, and, except at times when inter-community passions rise for particular reasons, there is a high degree of tolerance between Muslims and Christians and, generally speaking, Jews, although now there is only a small residual community of Jews surviving in Cairo and Alexandria.

A clear mark of this tolerance is the frequent juxtaposition of mosque and church in towns and villages throughout the land. It is certainly not the case that the 'temples' of the different faiths are planned to be in close proximity, but if the circumstances of community or topography lead to such religious neighbourliness it does not appear to be abhorrent to either side. If you travel the Nile by boat you cannot fail to see the minaret of the village mosque, crowned by the crescent, rise close to the double towers of the church, crowned with crosses. The two principal communities exist intermingled, if not integrated, the one with the other, and there are few outward signs to distinguish a Muslim from a Christian. To sincere believers of both faiths, the differences are important and indeed fundamental; but fundamentalism itself seems inappropriate in the Egyptian setting. The memories of the disputes and schisms of the early Church and of Islam must remind us that there can be no underestimating the passions that religion can engender even in a benign land like Egypt. But for the most part a deep community of interest inspires a fascinating and enviable coexistence between Muslims and Christians.

61 The central court of the school-
mosque (*madrasa*) of Sultan Hasan.
Built in the 14th century, it is
visually the most impressive mosque
in Cairo. The domed fountain in
the middle is probably not part of
the original mosque design.

Scribes, Calligraphy and the Word

Compare the flashing signs of Piccadilly Circus with those of the Midan el-Tahrir in Cairo, and you are at once struck by the elegance of the Arabic script. Even Coca-Cola looks good written in Arabic. Go to the Islamic Museum in Cairo and inspect some of the earliest Muslim tombstones with inscriptions written in the somewhat angular early Arabic script called Kufic; look at how it is used architecturally and decoratively in mosques, where figured embellishments in the Christian manner would be wholly improper - it is seen to specially good effect in, for example, the mosque of Ibn Tulun; observe how flexibly it can be used, adapted by lengthenings and compressions to fit available space. You do not need to be able to read it to appreciate its flexibility and its beauty. It has the smooth running grace of a script that is in essence to be written by hand. As such it is infinitely adaptable - you could say, the perfect script for advertising purposes - and needs to be written with style and strong variation. That is why, on the one hand, printed Arabic seems to be somewhat constrained, while, on the other, casually written Arabic is extremely difficult to read. It is not, one should declare, a script to be written casually, in the way that most Europeans now neglect penmanship. For it is the script of the Quran, and it forms an important element in the manner of diffusion of the Muslim faith.

There has been in Egypt since the Islamic invasion in the seventh century a devotion to the written word which has been not a passion for reading what is written (principally the Quran), but profound respect for the script itself, a respect

62 Naguib Mahfouz, winner of the Nobel Prize for literature in 1988 and the leading Egyptian novelist of Cairene life. Here he reads his newspaper in the Aly Baba café in the Midan el-Tahrir in the early morning, as he does most days.

63 *above* On the set of a television costume drama of medieval times, being recorded for transmission during the month of Ramadan. Cairo is the influential centre of Arab cinema and television production.

64 *below* A taxi-driver with his old taxi, waiting for a fare in Medinet el-Faiyum. Note the elegantly written Coca-Cola signs.

that does not extend to other forms of script. It has not followed that Egyptians have shown a burning desire to learn to read, any more than Europeans or the peoples of other cultures have done until relatively recent times. The situation has changed dramatically in the second half of the twentieth century, with the expansion of primary education in Egypt and the almost universal attendance of the young in schools. The practicalities of modern life have required more and more people, girls as well as boys, to learn the simple skills of reading and writing. To be able to use a pencil or pen is now a sign of accomplishment which a young person can set against the possibly modest learning of his parents and the almost certain illiteracy of his grandparents. There was in the 1960s a strange period of truth when visitors even to remote parts of Egypt, say, the island of Siheil south of Aswan, were assailed by crowds of small boys and girls demanding pencils and ball-point pens. It would not have happened in earlier times. What was even more surprising was to see these little things writing a few words on scraps of paper, not in Arabic but in English. The change from simple *bakhshish* to pencils was at the time devastating. Sadly now the demand for pencils has diminished, the idea of writing in an exotic script having ceased to be such a novelty.

Gauging the level of literacy in a community is difficult even if the community is capable of being questioned and assessed. For medieval and ancient times the task is almost impossible. What can one say of ancient Egypt? Extravagant claims have been made in the past by Egyptologists who have seemed to want to acquire credit for themselves by making the subjects of their studies more talented than they had evidence for. Why is it that a kind of sentimental lack of judgement will occasionally afflict a scholar who finds it hard to admit that his chosen protégés have weaknesses? But the Egyptians were not in fact particularly literate, although they did belong to a society which was distinctly literate. No visitor to Egypt can fail to wonder at the huge amount of inscriptional material embellishing the tombs and temples. No one who inspects the fine examples of papyri on view in the great collections of Egyptian antiquities can doubt that the ancient Egyptians were much given to putting things down in writing. The range is comprehensive within the limits of Egyptian culture; there is no history or philosophy in the modern, or even the Greek, senses, but there is much religion, literature, home-spun wisdom, mathematics, science (of a simple kind), medicine, and masses of everyday documents, private and public memoranda, letters, accounts, inventories, legal texts, reports. Writing was undoubtedly important for the Egyptians, and in the form of

65 The great international star of Egyptian cinema, Omar Sharif, looks down from a huge hoarding outside a cinema in Sharia Tala'at Harb (formerly Suliman Pasha Street) in the heart of fashionable Cairo.

66 *overleaf* A very fine example of Arabic calligraphy. Part of a Quran in seven volumes written in gold Thuluth script, copied by Mohamed ibn al-Wahid and illuminated by Mohamed ibn Mubadir and Aydughdi ibn Abd Allah el-Badri in 1304 for Rukn ed-Din Baybars, later the Sultan Baybars II (British Library, Add. 22406).

hieroglyphs was distinguished as being 'the words of the God'. The god is not specified, but should probably be identified as the sun-god Re. The idea of 'god' in the abstract was, it seems, comprehended by the Egyptians - the 'great god' without identification is often invoked - but for most Egyptians 'god' was actualised probably in the form of what was proper for the occasion, or thought to be suitable for the person concerned. The god of writing was Thoth, ibis-headed, he who ticked off the answers as you stood in awe suffering the viva-voce examination which would allow you to enter the realm of Osiris. But Thoth, the scribe before all scribes, was not necessarily the inventor of writing, of the words of the God. He certainly knew how to use them, and, if required, he would take down a letter for Re.

To be scribe in ancient Egypt was to be someone, and there was nothing derogatory in holding a title that the god Thoth held, and presumably was not ashamed to hold. A moment's thought will also remind one that the modern equivalent of 'scribe' is not just 'one who writes' - which is the strict translation - but 'secretary'; and a secretary can be anything from an honorary official of a golf-club, the right-hand assistant of a company director, the unwilling person who takes the minutes at the local charity meeting, to the Secretary of State for Foreign Affairs, a very senior minister of the Government. It was just so in ancient Egypt. You might be a lowly pen-pusher (or, to be more precise, brush-stroker), the official who looked after the estates for a king or a temple, or a very high official of the state. Nobody minded being called a scribe, and some of the greatest men of the land were very content to be shown in votive sculpture in the guise of a scribe, squatting on the ground with brush in hand and scribal equipment slung over the shoulder. It was good enough for General Horemheb, who became the last monarch of the Eighteenth Dynasty (*c.* 1319-1307 BC); for him, as an army commander under King Tutankhamun, it was more distinguished to be shown as a master of the peaceful profession than as a soldier. His career is a good example of how advancement might come in Egypt, from relative modesty to the crown itself. In Horemheb's case it cannot be said that being a scribe, or being shown to be a scribe, or having scribal titles was in the end the crucial factor in his preferment; but it was certainly no hindrance. With a scribe's equipment in your knapsack, you too might aspire to great things.

A proud person would certainly have viewed his son's prospects in this way, if he had successfully taken up the scribe's profession. 'Be a scribe' is the clarion call: be a scribe, and you are on the way to success. Apart from other advantages - a desk

بِسْمِ اللَّهِ الرَّحْمَٰنِ الرَّحِيمِ

وَالذَّارِيَاتِ ذَرْوًا فَالْحَامِلَاتِ وِقْرًا

فَالْجَارِيَاتِ يُسْرًا فَالْمُقَسِّمَاتِ أَمْرًا

إِنَّمَا تُوعَدُونَ لَصَادِقٌ وَإِنَّ الدِّينَ لَوَاقِعٌ

وَالسَّمَاءِ ذَاتِ الْحُبُكِ إِنَّكُمْ لَفِي قَوْلٍ

مُخْتَلِفٍ يُؤْفَكُ عَنْهُ مَنْ أُفِكَ قُتِلَ

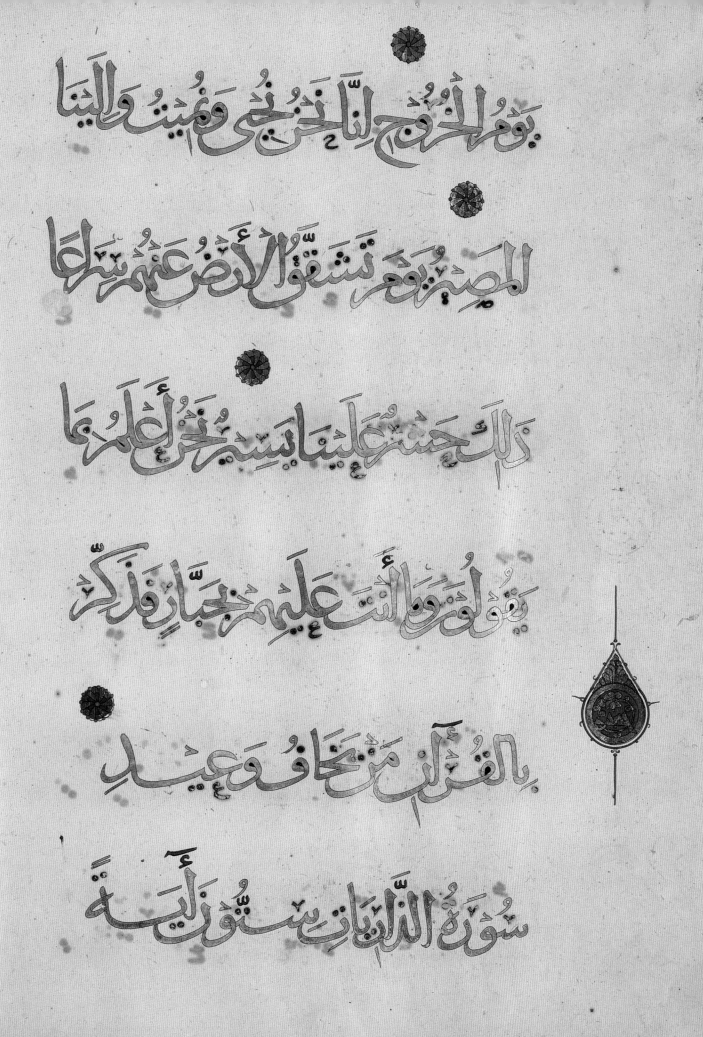

يَوْمُ الْخُرُوجِ لَنَا آخَرُ نَحْنُ نُحْيِى وَنُمِيتُ وَإِلَيْنَا

الْمَصِيرُ يَوْمَ تَشَقَّقُ الْأَرْضُ عَنْهُمْ سِرَاعًا

ذَٰلِكَ حَشْرٌ عَلَيْنَا يَسِيرٌ نَحْنُ أَعْلَمُ بِمَا

يَقُولُونَ وَمَا أَنْتَ عَلَيْهِم بِجَبَّارٍ فَذَكِّرْ

بِالْقُرْآنِ مَنْ يَخَافُ وَعِيدِ

سُورَةُ الذَّارِيَاتِ سِتُّونَ آيَةً

67 Queen Hatshepsut, shown as a king, runs a course in her symbolic jubilee festival: a block from the Red (quartzite) Chapel in the open-air museum at Karnak. The undetailed hieroglyphic signs of the texts are set out with a fine sense of space (Eighteenth Dynasty, c. 1465 BC).

job with immediate perks - there were other distinctly profitable implications: no military service (unless you were unlucky enough to be a military scribe), no call-up to the annual conscription for tidying up the land after the Nile flood; no taxes. A scribe was very much in command of his own life at the lowest level, and, because he could read and write, he could exercise subtle power over his fellows who might not be able to comprehend the scripts and work the calculating system. Scribes formed the Civil Service in ancient Egypt, and in more than one sense the case is the same today. A very large part of each year's crop of graduates from Egypt's universities become civil servants of one kind or another. Although many might hope to find jobs of a more lucrative kind, the security and certainty of the public service provide a safety net to catch all who fail to be placed elsewhere. It might be a job as a teacher in the crowded schools of the country; but more likely the graduate student migrates from lecture theatre to government office, to a lifetime of unchallenging work and much boredom. As in ancient times, the university degree provides a status and an entrée; but the prospects of advancement through the levels of administration to a position of significance are small, the competition is great, and the uncertainties of preferment many.

It must be supposed that prospects in antiquity were also very variable. Where enough information about families and careers can be gleaned from funerary and other records, it is clear that the young man who followed in his father's footsteps had a better chance of advancement than anyone setting out on his own to climb the ladder of preferment. The young scribe, learning his skills in a school or training scheme organised by a great temple or official bureau, would have little chance to choose his own route to fortune. If his talents were towards the use of the brush as a draughtsman or painter, and there were professional artists in his family, then he would surely spend his life working in the teams that provided the mural decorations in tombs and temples. If his abilities were turned to the skills of writing, administration or accounting, then, as likely as not, he would, again with the help of appropriate relations, end up in an office or agency. Some scribes who could write well and paint on a small scale might end up in the atelier where funerary texts were written, often illustrated with suitable little pictures, or vignettes, as they are commonly called. There were many niches for a scribe to occupy.

Most people who think about writing in ancient Egypt generally have the hieroglyphic script in mind. The handsome carved or painted signs used for monumental purposes and on a wide variety of object, both religious and secular, are in the

best cases elaborate, well-proportioned, carefully set out; they are formal and dignified. There are, of course, many exceptions to these 'best case' hieroglyphs, but in intention they should always be superior and special. Most writing in ancient Egypt, however, was not carried out in the hierophyphic script but in an abbreviated, cursive form called hieratic. Hieratic is not a priestly script, as the name suggests, but one which evolved from the earliest times, side by side with hieroglyphs, derived from them and designed for rapid use. It may be considered as a handwriting, and its relations to the formal hieroglyphs are as remote as - often more remote than - those of modern handwriting to formal printed texts. The essential scribal script, hieratic developed its own practices in forms and spellings over the centuries, and in the hands of competent scribes came to bear little resemblance to its formal ancestor. In its final stage, as a script called demotic, the resemblances have almost totally vanished. The distinction between demotic and hieroglyphic is clearly observable in the central and top bands of text on the Rosetta Stone, written respectively in demotic and hieroglyphic; they convey essentially the same basic text, but in script and even in grammatical forms they are so unlike each other that the early decipherers of the stone's inscriptions were much puzzled. The demotic script, like hieratic, was not intended to be carved on stone, and the existence of a few carved texts demonstrates not only this unsuitability but also the good reasons why hieratic and demotic were developed for writing with a rush brush, quickly and informally on papyrus, wood or pottery, and only occasionally on stone.

Good professional scribes, writing formal documents, were masters of their skills. The best scribes developed very stylish hands, writing with confidence and *élan*, introducing bold forms, often apparently for effect, embellishing their writing with flourishes and extended contours, using exaggerated shapes and running ligatures; such distinguish the work of individual scribes and of particular periods of writing. Religious texts on papyrus are written very carefully in styles of hieratic script that are very regular and clear, as if intended to be helpful to the person for whom the text might have been written out. A copy of the *Book of the Dead* buried with its owner in his tomb would be an important aid to his posthumous existence. There is every likelihood that the tomb-owner, great official though he might be, would not have been able in life to read the text; but in death the papyrus could by magic become his required bedside book, and, if carefully written, would be so much more readable. No such care was needed for any document written for the living, for these were written by scribes to be read by scribes. It should be no surprise to find

68 Brown quartzite block statue of the high scribal official Tetity, from Karnak (Eighteenth Dynasty, c. 1450 BC). The block statue form provided fine surfaces for the accommodation of dedicatory texts (British Museum, 888).

that writing in antiquity was a professional activity, and that in consequence the reading of what was written was equally a task for the specialist. There is some evidence that high officials may have had some competence in literacy in the Late Period, but their abilities may not have extended much beyond writing their own names. Even that may be doubted. A fine document in The Brooklyn Museum contains a series of witness statements made by some of the highest Theban officials of the time (651 BC). Each is written in a different hand, and it has been suggested, very reasonably, that each is an actual autograph of the high official concerned. It is unfortunately equally a possibility that the statements were written by each official's personal scribe.

In the bulk of documents surviving on papyrus from ancient Egypt the preponderance of religious texts is noticeable, but it is certain that scribal activities were principally concerned with secular documents. The survival of the casual productions of daily life, of letters, notes, accounts, is chancy; such writings are by nature ephemeral. Legal documents and official reports, on the other hand, were conceived of as having longer archival lives, and they have survived in larger numbers when the circumstances for preservation have been favourable. Papyrus is an exceptionally tough and durable writing material if it is not subjected to damp conditions over a long period or to fire, or is not invaded by destructive insects. Texts in tombs have a far better chance of natural survival unless they are destroyed by the hand of man. The quantities of secular writings that have survived can only represent a minuscule part of the output of the armies of scribes who were hard at work from the time of the earliest dynasties. Some chance discovery may yet transform the picture, but the possibilities diminish as ancient town sites are destroyed by the activities of modern life or by the rise of subsoil water. The huge and diverse collections of papyri, mostly written in Greek and found in the rubbish dumps of towns in the Faiyum and in Middle Egypt, in particular at Oxyrhynchus and Hermopolis, show what can survive under less than best conditions. At Qasr Ibrim in Egyptian Nubia, the arid nature of the place has preserved masses of texts on papyrus, vellum and even paper, covering the periods from the Graeco-Roman to the eighteenth century AD. Dryness and the absence of the human hand are best for papyrus survival, but are less sustainable today, for even the lack of rain in Upper Egypt and Nubia is less constant than formerly, since the building of the High Dam and the massive evaporation of water from Lake Nasser cause subsequent precipitation in the south.

69 *above* The scribe Hunefer shown in his *Book of the Dead* meeting his judgement in the afterlife: his record is tested, his answers are noted by ibis-headed Thoth, god of writing, and he is led to Osiris by Horus (Nineteenth Dynasty, c. 1300 BC; British Museum, 9901).

70 *below* A bold stylish hand distinguishes the hieratic text of the Great Harris Papyrus, a document listing the benefactions of King Ramesses III to the temples of Egypt (Twentieth Dynasty, c. 1170 BC; British Museum, 9999).

Of the surviving texts written on papyrus, some of the most interesting are private letters; in their personal communication they bring us close to particular individuals and have a human quality which is usually absent from more formal documents. It is worth a little time to consider not only their content but also the manner of their production. Although there are some surviving letters which are packed with information, personal and general, the majority are characterised by little information and a deal of formality; they are mostly carefully structured, making use of a kind of proforma of content in which the emphasis is on the structure provided by address, greetings and conclusion. A typical ancient letter will spend most of its space on the formalities. Greetings at great length, invocations of the gods for good health and safety, confine the crucial matter of the letter, perhaps a piece of useful information or an instruction to the recipient to do something, to a few lines. If the reader is not on the *qui vive*, there is always the risk of missing the point of a letter, just as one may miss the filling of an over-pastried pie. The same phenomenon can be found in letters written in Egypt today - not letters written by educated, literate people, but those sent as duty or 'bread-and-butter' communications by servants, workmen and others who will have employed a professional letter-writer. It seems to be the principal characteristic of the letter written by a hired scribe on behalf of a client who cannot read and cannot argue against the extension of the length of his letter for reasons of form. The scribe's purpose may not be wholly without self-interest; a letter is paid for by length, and an elaborate framework consisting mostly of conventional elements guarantees a letter of a certain minimum length. There is also a kind of satisfaction in having a letter written on your behalf by someone who knows what the correct forms are. In simple societies conformity with convention is very important; the right procedures make the outcome more secure.

Nothing much is known about the village scribe in ancient Egypt. He may have been someone who for some reason was unable to hold an official position, or who had lost his job. In some communities there were no doubt scribes enough in regular posts who were prepared to do a little extra work on the side. But the writing of a letter must always have been something of an occasion, for Egyptians were no great travellers and there were only irregular arrangements for the delivery of letters other than official communications. If a letter were written, shall we suppose, in Thebes to someone living in Siut (Asyut) in Middle Egypt, the writer would have to find someone who was going downstream and would be prepared to deliver the letter to some responsible official in Siut, who would then ensure that it reached the addressee. There may have been better-organised procedures, but the evidence for such has not survived. In modern Egypt there are undoubtedly local letter-writers who undertake to prepare a letter for a client for a fee. It was formerly not uncommon to see such hired scribes at work in or near the local coffee-house in a village or town, and the more successful practitioners might even have had type-writers. A letter by typewriter costs more than one by hand; and if it has to be written in English or some other European language, a different tariff applies. The client has no way of ensuring that the resulting letter, especially if it is in a language other than Arabic, will be couched in the best terms. A very good example of such a letter, written to Howard Carter by his foreman, provides the form, minimal content and interesting style which are characteristic of letters written by illiterate employees. In this letter, written on 5 August 1923, the hand of the scribe is rather accomplished, one that would not have disgraced a well-educated person:

> Honourable Sir,
> Begts write this letter hoping that you are enjoying good health, and ask the Almighty to keep you and bring you back in Safety.
> Begts inform your Excellency that Store No.15 is alright, Treasure is alright, the Northern Store is alright, Wadain and House are all alright, and in all your Work order is carried on according to your honourable instructions.
> Rais Hussein, Gad Hassan, Hassan Awad Abdelah Ahmed and all the Gaffirs of the house beg to send their best regards.
> My best regards to you respectable Self, and all members of the Lord's family, and all your friends in England.
> Longing to your early coming,
> Your most obedient servant
> Rais Ahmed Gurgar

The work of the local scribe stands at the lower end of the output of the scribal hierarchy. It is undoubtedly the case that the very best scribes - and here we mean not officials with scribal titles but those who actually wielded brush and ink on papyrus - were employed in the service of the king, the high officers of state (in effect, again the king) and the great temples. The surviving royal documents like the reports on tomb robberies in the Twentieth and Twenty-First Dynasties and the Great Harris Papyrus are calligraphic *tours de force*. The last of these (in the British Museum), the longest of surviving papyri at 41 metres (134 ft) and containing a comprehensive account of the donations of King Ramesses III (*c.* 1194 - 1163 BC) to the temples throughout Egypt, sustains a remarkable uniformity of script from start to finish. The hand is bold, full of graceful flourishes, with dramatic use of elongated tall signs and extended horizontal signs; there are many joined groups (ligatures), but the general effect is one of striking clarity. It is as if the whole text were written by the same scribe, although common sense would suggest the sharing of the task between several scribes whose hands were so similar that they appear like one. Particularly bold writing characterises the beginnings of sections, and this form of emphasis was common in documents of the New Kingdom and later. It was not so much so in earlier times, although a strange and dramatic elongation of signs is found in the first few lines of early Middle-Kingdom letters, in these cases probably used both as a space-filling device and a demonstration of scribal flamboyance.

In this use of large, florid signs at the start of texts we can observe perhaps the very earliest employment of exaggerated forms which later becomes so regular both in the writing of Arabic texts and in the preparation of Western medieval manuscripts. There is a thought here which could possibly bear further examination. In the monumental texts of ancient Egypt, carried out in the hieroglyphic script, there was no tradition of marking the beginnings of important inscriptions with specially large signs. In general, within a text of whatever importance, strict regularity was maintained in the laying out of lines and in the quadratic disposition of signs. The beauty of a hieroglyphic text lay as much in this regularity of form and of spacing as in the care with which the individual signs were designed and carved. A text made up of well-ordered but simply cut undetailed signs can provide an aesthetic satisfaction almost as great as that of a text in which each sign is a small decorative masterpiece. The discipline of hieroglyphs is very different from the freedom of the hieratic script, and the good scribe could exploit this freedom through his skill in manipulating the forms. A fine hand has its special aesthetic appeal, and it is true in Egypt for the hieratic and demotic scripts, for the fine, regular, rounded scripts used for the best Greek texts and, by descent, for the splendid liturgical manuscripts of the Copts. The tradition, although not one of direct transmission, is especially evident in Arabic manuscripts, and, in a particular way, in later

71 *above* Porters carry a framed landscape of a somewhat un-Egyptian scene and an elaborately written and mounted Quranic text; in front of a new mosque in Luxor.

72 *below* A priest as jackal-headed Anubis, god of embalming, puts the finishing touches to the mummy of Sennedjem, one of the artist-craftsmen of the community at Deir el-Medina (Nineteenth Dynasty, *c.* 1200 BC).

Turkish texts of the Ottoman occupation. In all the 'stages' of this continuing series of writing traditions, the use of exaggerated forms contrasts markedly with their absence in the carved monumental texts in stone of the same stages. Regularity in carving, flamboyance in writing.

The written word is so taken for granted in modern times that one tends to forget how magical is the idea of transmitting spoken material through a written medium. What is initially something to be heard becomes something to be read and comprehended. There is, of course, a further complication which can no longer be appreciated today; that is the extent to which people in antiquity who could read, did in fact read quietly, that is without enunciating what they read out loud. We may all be familiar with children who, in the early stages of reading, speak what they read, mouthing the words as if to give themselves confidence. It has been said that Alexander the Great was the first recorded person to have read quietly, but it is unlikely that he discovered the technique. In the ancient Egyptian language you 'heard' a letter, you did not 'read' it; but this usage reflects the practical fact that few recipients of letters would have been able to read the written sheet. If an Egyptian were faced with a sign at the entrance to a sacred enclosure, stating, presumably in the hieroglyphic script, 'Keep out! Sacred ibis pens', would he speak the words, or simply take in the message? Today, if you were alone, the message would be absorbed quietly; if you were with others, you might well read it out aloud. So, surely, it would have been in antiquity, especially if your companion were not literate. In general, however, it must be supposed that writing was intended for reading aloud. The dead presumably sat up in their coffins to read the contents of the religious papyri buried with them; it seems unlikely that it was thought that they could simply absorb the messages without opening the papyrus rolls. At the time of burial, one of the acts in the drama of interment was the opening of the bodily vents - the eyes, ears, nose, mouth - to allow the dead person to make use of the faculties associated with them, including seeing and speaking.

On the basis of very little evidence, it is maintained that much of the scribal training was carried out by rote, by dictation, by spoken repetition, by memorising large pieces of suitable texts. The recovery of many examples of excerpts from a relatively few well-known compositions suggests the persistence of a kind of national curriculum of recommended books. There existed in antiquity an attachment to certain literary texts which lasted for hundreds of years, but there is no evidence of a universal acceptance of any specific religious texts crucial to belief.

The Word itself was venerated, and the ability to repeat particular sacred texts according to your particular religious allegiances, to write and to read them, was certainly important. There was no single body of religious texts like the Bible and the Quran that commanded special veneration as a divinely inspired corpus. In a sense, therefore, the young in their training were not so tied to the specifics of textual integrity as their Christian and Muslim descendants; time could in consequence be concentrated on the acquisition of essential scribal skills, of writing, composing, copying, calculating.

The continuities in learning traditions which were found in Coptic and Muslim schools until fairly recent times have to a great extent been modified by the need to widen the range of subjects taught to children; the pressures of the modern world require more than an intimate knowledge of religious texts. In recent years, however, the intensification of devotional emphases in religious practices may well lead to a revival of the importance given, in some schools at least, to the old practices of learning and reciting parts of the Bible and the Quran on a regular and more intensive basis. The schools which Lane observed in Cairo in the mid-nineteenth century were very limited in what they offered and at what they aimed. Writing was not a priority; but learning by heart selected texts, mostly religious, took up most of the time. This method was to some extent based on the tradition which was most completely followed in the great Muslim university of El-Azhar in Cairo. Here, in the greatest centre of religious instruction in the Islamic world, instruction was mostly carried out by sheikhs with small groups of students, squatting on mats in the great court and its surrounding arcades - as indeed it still is, but to a lesser extent than formerly. The teaching was almost wholly oriented towards Islam, and all subjects, including law and mathematics, were heavily biased towards religious purposes. There was in the strict cursus of full instruction an indulgence towards time which required up to fifteen years for total completion. Such a leisurely approach does not suit present-day requirements. But there can be no doubt that in forms of education which lay great stress on spiritual matters, supported by close examination of religious texts, things ought not to be rushed; instruction includes a maturing process, and a long application to study is more likely to ensure that a student who has completed the whole cycle will emerge with a confident certainty in his own learning. So it can be achieved if the goals are properly defined, as they have been traditionally in Egypt. It is good still to find a country in which people respect the learned, honour the ability to write, and revere the Word.

73 Morning school is over, and in the village of Ezbet Bashendi in the oasis of El-Dakhla young Mohamed may dream of becoming a civil servant.

Chapter 7

The Bureaucratic Web

It used to be said that wherever you went in Egypt, and whatever you wanted to do, it was always advisable to have the right piece of paper - to open doors, to confirm permissions, to establish authority, and simply just to get things done. It was also suggested that a piece of paper with an official-looking stamp was quite enough, for the likelihood would be that the first person to look at it - the *bowab* on the gate - would not be able to read, and would let you through. It was not true, at least as far as the second supposition was concerned. But it is true that the right written document can be a real *laisser-passer* in Egypt today. The skills of the scribe, writing and reading, commemorated in the last chapter, are generally considered to be the fundamental requirements for a decent education. Unfortunately, you might say, they are also crucial for the development of bureaucracy; and its bureaucracy has since time immemorial been an outstanding characteristic of Egypt.

A study of the history of Egypt in the first two dynasties in the early third millennium BC shows that when written texts first appeared, there was already established a well-organised system of administration. There were officers of state, local officials, papyrus documents - the makings, in fact, of a bureaucracy on national and local levels. Among the earliest written evidence are the sealings placed on jars, boxes and bags, stamped with the names of kings, the sources of the contents, the titles and perhaps the names of officials. These impressions, applied by cylinder seals, were weighty authentifications of authority, that of the king in particular, and of his officials by delegation. In addition, from the same period come the

74 Coffin-lid of Sisobk, northern vizier of Egypt in the reign of Psammetichus I (Twenty-Sixth Dynasty, c. 650 BC). The vizier epitomised the bureaucratic administration of Egypt, and took responsibility for all official activities on behalf of his monarch. From Memphis (British Museum,17).

earliest cursive texts, the beginnings of hieratic writing, consisting of notations on pottery vessels and identificatory notes on wooden labels. These brief notes demonstrate that cursive writing started almost as soon as the hieroglyphic script began to develop; the cursive satisfied a need for speed and convenience, and it was used especially for bureaucratic purposes.

It is not easy to formulate a clear picture of how matters advanced in the way of writing and officialdom in those early centuries, nearly five thousand years ago, because almost the totality of surviving evidence comes from tombs; funerary evidence is not only one-sided, but also limited in range. The discovery of more tombs tends only to increase the bulk of inscribed material, but not its variety. Even so, this one-sided evidence shows clearly that the use of writing was largely prompted by the need to record and to account. What is in this jar, or in this box? How many items are there? Where does the wine come from? Who is the tomb-owner, or the king in whose reign he lived? Writing was in its inception rather a banal, though imaginative, tool for practical purposes. How much more satisfactory if it had been devised to record the noble inventions of heroic poets! It was not so; it was to help the bureaucracy to keep accounts of persons and things, and the dreadful thought occurs that the 'words of the God' of the hieroglyphic script were not created by the great god himself but by some bright echelon of scribes in the royal city of Memphis. It must be supposed that the principle of recording numbers by using simple strokes was not hard to conceive; and the principle of indicating, shall we say, a pot or pair of sandals, by drawing a conventional pot-shape or the outline of sandals, would also have been a simple development. So, the method of recording at the lowest level would not have been beyond the wit of a bright young official to introduce. The steps by which drawings of things came to be used to represent sounds and then to spell out whole words, by which the idea arose that actions as well as things could be indicated, and by which what we call 'sentences' conveying more than simple statements could be expressed visually through the same system of signs, are all unknown and now beyond reconstruction. It is not too imaginative, perhaps, to consider the high level of intellectual excitement that must have existed in the ranks of officials, especially, no doubt, those of the middle and lower ranks - the ones at the sharp end of administration - during the years of literate development. Can it have happened that particular individuals would bring forward clever ideas for consideration? It must have been so. The modern idea of committee consensus could scarcely be applied to the primitive evolution of acceptable practices

75 King Sethos II offers papyrus bouquets to falcon-headed Monthu, the ancient deity of Thebes. A scene on the rear wall of the king's triple barque shrine in the Great Court of the Karnak Temple (Nineteenth Dynasty, c. 1210 BC).

five thousand years ago. Ideas may have come from abroad, or have been generated locally, but it may be supposed that those who first conceived and then developed the Egyptian system of writing did so for severely practical purposes, and had no conception of what writing would eventually come to.

This somewhat commonplace view of the beginning of writing as a tool of officialdom is supported by the evidence for the use of papyrus as a writing material in the earliest dynasties. A discovery of a fibrous material in a First-Dynasty tomb at Saqqara just before the Second World War has been claimed as the first physical confirmation of papyrus use at this early time. There is still some doubt about the identification of this material as a manufactured writing medium, and no ink marks were found on it at the time of discovery. But the existence in the First Dynasty of papyrus and papyrus rolls is in any case virtually certain; some of the tiny texts in cylinder seal impressions include a sign which is clearly the earliest form of one which in later times represents a roll of papyrus, tied up and sealed. What were rolls of papyrus used for at this time? The romantic might consider the possibility of early versions of the religious texts - prayers, mythical expositions, divine statements - which do not otherwise appear until they are found in hiero-glyphic form as Pyramid Texts, the exclusively royal compositions carved on the walls of the inner chambers of pyramids of the late Fifth Dynasty and subsequently. Much more probably, the early papyri carried records of simple activities and in-ventories of goods, set out in lists and tabular form. The earliest inscribed papyri that have survived are all of this kind. They can be dated to the late Fourth Dynasty (from Gebelein) and Fifth Dynasty (especially from Abusir). They have been found in the neighbourhood of religious foundations, but are wholly bureaucratic in pur-pose. The majority of them record duties and lists of equipment used in daily and periodic rituals. There seems to be no other conclusion than that the initial spur for the invention of writing in Egypt and the stimulus for development came from the ranks of officialdom, who could see in such a system ways of establishing with accuracy what otherwise could only be recorded by memory, and of setting down details of things that could then be read and confirmed by others at a later date and without the presence of an individual exercising memory.

It may be supposed that the advantages of writing would have been appreciated by others who would have seen what officialdom was doing. If you can note down the contents of a jar, you can also mention a simple historical fact. An ivory label from Abydos, now in the British Museum, shows King Den striking a fallen enemy with a mace. The little scene is briefly described in hieroglyphs as 'the first striking of the Asiatic'; this interpretation of the simple First-Dynasty signs seems certain. It is a short step from such a beginning to develop a tabulation of important events, an annalistic exposition of history of the kind found on a slab known as the Palermo Stone (no matter what date should be assigned to that fascinating record). Tabulations are essentially listings, and may also be properly considered as bureaucratically inspired. So we must think, in the absence of other evidence, that writing developed as the primary tool of Egyptian officials, and that from the earliest historical times the writer, the scribe, the bureaucrat, established a firm grip on the administration of the country which has never been relaxed.

The piece of paper with a prominent stamp on it, which was mentioned at the beginning of this chapter, is symbolic of the state of affairs today just as much as the little papyrus roll sent from a Nubian fort to Thebes in the Twelfth Dynasty; in the case of the latter, its mud-sealing would be impressed with the device engraved on the signet scarab of the appropriate official and recognisable as a sign of authenticity and authority, the very equivalent of the rubber-stamp impression. Every government that has controlled life in Egypt from the time of the earliest dynasties down to the present day has continued the bureaucratic regime of the land, each one usually adding to and complicating what preceded. The Pharaonic period sustained the innovations of the first administrators in the native tradition, down to the Alexandrian conquest and the subsequent Macedonian-Greek rule. The habits and practices of the mainly urban Greeks, subjected to the authoritarian governance of the Ptolemaic successors to the Pharaohs, resulted in a substantial spread of civic administration, generating a flood of paperwork which seems to have been willingly accepted by the Egyptian population; they had already by the fourth century BC become accustomed to the requirements of Egyptian bureaucracy in the form of lavish documentation. Among surviving secular texts on papyrus from the whole of the pre-Christian period, a very large proportion consists of legal contracts set out on very generous sheets of papyrus and often for what now seems to have been trivial purposes. A good, but incomplete, example dated in the sixth year of Alexander, son of Alexander the Great (311 BC), is a sheet which was originally about 2.80 metres long and 0.39 metres wide (9 ft × 1 ft 3 in); it bears five copies of a contract for the cession of a house in Thebes, written out in long lines of text, each well over one metre (3 ft) in length, and quite hopelessly disposed for convenient reading. More than two-thirds of the papyrus surface is left blank. It has

76 One of the earliest hieroglyphic documents: this ivory tablet shows King Den striking a fallen foreigner, and the signs on the right read 'the first occasion of smiting the East(erner)'; from Abydos (First Dynasty, c. 2825 BC; British Museum, 55586).

all the characteristics of a legal document of almost any culture, in which the system has overtaken the convenience and interest of the client. The substance of the text, although no doubt of importance to the people concerned - to Kollouthes, his mother Taneferhotep and the woman Taesis, who cede the house to the woman Nitocris - seems scarcely worthy of such an impressively produced instrument. The scribal lawyers of the time could have learned little from modern solicitors.

Such huge and unnecessarily expensive documents - for papyrus was never a commodity cheaply come by in antiquity - demonstrate very clearly the extent to which the ancient official class of Egypt held its defenceless people in bureaucratic thrall. There was, probably, some encouragement from the side of the client, for an impressive document proved that the issue was important, and there was also a substantial product to show for the expense incurred. And so the process continued through the Roman Imperial Period, which in time moved into the Byzantine rule of Constantinople - 'Byzantine' is itself a byword for convoluted, tortuous administration. Two texts which interestingly perpetuate the Christian-Byzantine tradition in the context of Islamic Egypt are the letters-testimonial from the Coptic Patriarch to the Christian community in Nubia announcing the consecration of Timotheos as the new Nubian bishop, whose seat was at Qasr Ibrim. The texts, one in Coptic and one in Arabic, demonstrate the linguistic realities of the time, Coptic being the liturgical language of the Church and Arabic the vernacular, in which services were probably already conducted, as they still are in the present-day Coptic Church of Egypt. The letters were written after Timotheos' consecration in the famous El-Muallaqa ('hanging') church in Old Cairo in AD 1371-2. Both are on paper scrolls nearly five metres long, and show the fine calligraphy of both scripts, with splendid initial elaborations of the kind mentioned in the last chapter. These two magnificent documents are perhaps not in the best sense examples of bureaucracy at work in daily life; but they do show that the practices of scribal domination were equally pervasive in the Christian religious field at a time when the land was predominantly Muslim. Forms and traditions die hard; in this case there is no sign of any terminal decline.

The remarkable physical conditions which have allowed such a fragile material as paper to survive in the fortress site of Qasr Ibrim in Nubia have also secured the preservation of many ephemeral documents of later times, mostly of the seventeenth and eighteenth centuries, which illustrate the modest legal transactions of the remote, almost abandoned, garrison of Ottoman troops who occupied the place.

77 Kamal Ashaqy Hafaz with his horse and carriage (*arabiya* or *garri*) outside the offices of the National Democratic Party in the Sharia en-Nil in Luxor. The offices occupy a fine villa built in the French colonial style of the late 19th and early 20th centuries.

The little documents, also written on paper, record the legal arrangements for land transfers, sales of palm trees, sales of commodities, etc., the small activities of daily life which presumably helped to relieve the tedium of service on the southern frontier of the Ottoman Empire. In them is none of the expansive display of the Theban contracts of nearly two thousand years earlier. Such modest documentation seems right for an outpost where, in contrast to metropolitan Thebes, there may have been only a handful of officials who could even read and write. The virtual exiles of Qasr Ibrim were, in their isolation and comparative security from central authority, in much better state than most native Egyptians at the time. Until the late nineteenth century, when the corrupt and partial administration of the land was reorganised and made reasonably just by European administrators working for the Khedivial government, the bureaucratic regime of Egypt had lost those aspects of control and legality which had sustained it throughout antiquity and for many centuries later. With better administration, bureaucracy flourished, and the legacy of the new order remains a triumph of proper management in which almost anything can be achieved with the right piece of paper.

People who have travelled widely are impressed by the complexity and importance of documentation in modern Egypt, the unconscionable delays and the inability to keep appointments. The heart of Egyptian bureaucracy lies in the forbidding maze of the Mogama'a building in Cairo. You go to the Mogama'a for all kinds of official permissions, for travel documents, if you are an Egyptian citizen, for visas and renewals of visas, if you are a foreigner. It is said that people become lost in the labyrinthine corridors of its many floors, overcome by desperation, by weariness, by the utter dreariness of its undecorated rooms, by the seemingly endless search for the appropriate official. And yet, in spite of all, things go on ticking; somehow the administration does not grind to a halt. Give it rather more than half a chance, and you may find that you are stepping out successfully clutching your piece of paper, into the sunlight of the Midan el-Tahrir, Liberation Square - well-named at such a moment - with the Egyptian Museum beckoning you a few hundred yards away, with a torrent of traffic and a mêlée of buses between.

If only you can control your impatience and retain some sweetness of temperament, your predicament may well be relieved by those very catch-words which for most people encapsulate the Egyptian bureaucracy: *ma'aleesh* (not so much 'it doesn't matter' as 'may it turn out well in the end') and *bukra* ('tomorrow'), the verbal panaceas so seriously misunderstood by most foreigners. Both these words convey,

78 *above* A model wooden granary containing figures of four workmen and a scribe taking records of the amounts of grain stored; a typical object found in the tombs at Beni Hasan in Middle Egypt (Twelfth Dynasty, c. 1850 BC; British Museum, 41573).

79 *below* Goose-herds bring forward their flock of geese, with goslings in baskets, to be presented to Nebamun, whose tomb was in the Theban Necropolis. A scribe from the estate presents the goose account (Eighteenth Dynasty, c. 1375 BC; British Museum, 37978).

with characteristic Egyptian tact, apology, hope, and encouragement. And how much better to be told *bukra* than *abadan* ('never'). The technique of gentle delay is well understood by Egyptians themselves. The sad knots of people thronging the Mogama'a building know that to wait may mean to succeed. Waiting is almost a national pastime, in bus stations, in railway stations, in airports, in offices for almost any petition or request. If you are too important or too busy to wait yourself, then there is always someone else who will wait for you, and either transact your business by proxy or summon you in the nick of time. It is the ancient principle of the deputy, always available to the person of influence or good position. In antiquity it might have been necessary to have someone who would fulfil the duties required under conscription at the time of the rehabilitation of the countryside from the destructive effects of the Nile flood. By extension you could make the same provision for your after-life by having a *shabti*-figure or two buried with you, to be activated if the call-up caught you. In more recent times the infamous *corvée*, used in effect to press-gang villagers for public works and military service, could be circumvented either by bribing the appropriate official or by maiming the potential subject so that he would be of no use for heavy physical work. A young man might, for example, have his trigger-finger cut off so that he could not be used in the army. It was one of the triumphs of Sir Evelyn Baring, the first British diplomatic agent and consul-general in Egypt, to suppress the practice in the late nineteenth century. The *corvée* has long gone, but it is still possible for the poor labourer or inexperienced farmer to be exploited on the local level.

Exploitation by an unsympathetic bureaucracy is one of the more noticeable continuities in Egypt, although very much less evident today than it was up to a hundred years ago. Many writings have survived from ancient Egypt which show what miserable lives most people lived, partly because of the disagreeable nature of their professions and substantially because they could be exploited by the scribes who ran the administration. The compositions produced in the New Kingdom to glorify the scribal profession, and to be used apparently as writing exercises by student scribes, are full of one-sided accounts, the main theme of which is how much better it is to be a scribe than anything else. The scribe escapes most of the problems of daily life which afflict most men, and they are often on the side of oppressive authority when force is used. The plight of the farmer is particularly emphasised. It is the scribe who makes the assessment for taxation on crops in advance of the harvest; it is the scribe who determines what has to be handed over in the form of grain and other commodities; it is the scribe who comes along with the Egyptian equivalent of the bailiff's men, to enforce the official extortions, to inflict punishment and to feel very self-righteous at being on the right side of the law.

As the surviving written record on papyrus has, of necessity, been written by scribes, and as the scenes and inscriptions in tombs are again laid out by scribes, it is not surprising that what is read and seen about ancient Egypt is monstrously biased in favour of this profession. The bland statements of fair treatment to the poor and the underprivileged which form a large part of the substance of Egyptian wisdom literature fall, therefore, within the limits of what officialdom conceived as being proper. The sentiments are good, but the implementation of policies based on such sentiments is quite another matter. There is not much doubt that ordinary people in antiquity had a pretty tough time; in this, one should say, Egypt was not particularly exceptional in the ancient or medieval worlds. But it takes some close examination of visual and written evidence to appreciate the wretchedness of the common lot. The full nastiness is not, however, properly depicted, because a tomb-scene, for example, represents a kind of ideal situation, in farm, field or workshop, in which the deceased tomb-owner would expect to pass his life after death. Squalor does not form a very acceptable subject for representation in these circumstances; but it does not take much imagination to conceive the conditions under which farm-workers and craftsmen carried out their duties, whether or not they were being closely watched by the ever-present scribal official or thumped by the officers of the law for great or small misdemeanours. Tax-defaulters, for example, are depicted being brought forward, backs bowed in submission, ready to receive the blows of the officious attendants who lead them to the presence of the senior official to whom the defaulters owe their allegiance and the attendants their services.

A chilling picture of disadvantage is painted by the author of a composition known generally as the *Satire of Trades*. Although it survives only in copies from the New Kingdom, it was probably composed in the early Middle Kingdom, a seminal period of thought and literary development in Egypt. The author's name may be Dua-Khety, or possibly Khety son of Duauf. His purpose is to show how much better off a scribe is than anyone else - the theme we have already mentioned. 'Whatever job a scribe has in town, he will not be disadvantaged'; being a scribe is 'the best of all professions - nothing could be better in the land'. Even in his early days of training a scribe might be entrusted with important errands; whoever would send a carver or a goldsmith? Consider the lot of the blacksmith with hands like a crocodile's, and

80 Ramses Square by the main railway station in Cairo. A colossal statue of Ramesses II from ancient Memphis dominates the scene. In his long reign (c.1290-1224 BC) Egyptian bureaucracy achieved new heights of complexity.

smelling of fish. Carpenters are worn out by using tools; the gem-cutter suffers from eye-strain and bad back. And so the catalogue continues. The potter is filthy, puddling his clay; the mason is exhausted and covered with dust; the gardener's neck is swollen with carrying the yoke; the weaver is cramped in his work, sees little of the daylight, and is flogged if he takes a day off; the courier in the desert faces lions and Asiatics; the fisherman has crocodiles to contend with. The author, with some complacency, comes to his final section: only scribes are free from supervision; every trade is worse than the other; a farmer is not a man. So it behoves a scribe to watch his behaviour, to honour his parent, respect authority, ape the great; consider well the good fortune that decided at the time of his birth that he would be a scribe. At the last, one reads with a certain disgust, 'It has come to a good end'.

The contemptuous tone of the *Satire of Trades* represents, without a doubt, the continuing attitude of government officials to those who have little to support them and no one to take up their cases. For efficiency in tax-gathering and, in

consequence, of oppression and exploitation, the Roman adminstration in the early centuries AD was probably unparalleled. The Emperor Augustus instituted a census, regularly adjusted and renewed, which enabled the imperial bureaucracy to keep a far tighter grip on the Egyptian and Greek residents of the country than had ever been the case previously. As substantial quantities of produce and of revenue were regularly remitted to Rome, the need to maximise collection was extreme, and contractors were used for the purpose. Complaints were received that unauthorised taxes were often levied, that farmers were in no position to challenge unlawful demands and were sometimes obliged to run away to avoid summary punishment for non-payment. Generally speaking, however, the elaborate system of bureaucratic government maintained from Imperial into Byzantine times ensured an efficiency and overall control which, it is said, survived into the years following the Arab conquest. That does not mean that the regime was necessarily equitable, or bearable to the simple peasant. Servility seems to have been the accepted attitude to

81 The well-planned village of the royal necropolis workmen at Deir el-Medina in the Theban hills. This community of literate people developed its own local bureaucracy. The little reconstructed pyramid in the foreground marks a tomb-chapel (c. 1500-1000 BC).

authority, and so it continued right down to the nineteenth century. Under Mohammed Ali, Pasha of Egypt, rural oppression was extreme and extended far beyond what was authorised by central government. Lane pointed out that 'even the Sheykh of a village, in executing the commands of his superiors, abuses his lawful powers: bribes, and the ties of relationship and marriage influence him and them, and by lessening the oppression of some, who are more able to bear it, greatly increase that of others'. And even the headman is often beaten worse than others if the village fails to meet its quota. 'All the fella'heen are proud of the stripes they receive for withholding their contributions, and are often heard to boast of the number of blows which were inflicted upon them before they would give up their money.'

Times have indeed greatly changed, but suspicion of officials remains. During the First World War, when peasants received unprecedented prices for their crops, a peculiar situation developed. Howard Carter pointed out in a letter to a friend that the government was having to issue five-piastre notes because all the silver coin was being secretly hoarded below ground in the villages of Egypt. Central government bureaucracy was engrossed with other matters, and a state of semi-anarchy prevailed in the countryside. Where all control is seen to be bad control, how do you instil a respect for the official, the scribe, the bureaucrat? A human face helps; a sympathetic ear inspires confidence; above all, a sense of humour, especially when matters look bad, can often win the day. If a man pursuing some problem in a public office can make the official laugh, then he may be within reach of success. Further, if the bureaucracy itself, or its products, can be shown to be subjects of unmalicious fun, then anything is achievable. For bureaucracy as such should be able to look after itself. Years ago, when things were still difficult in Egypt, new controls were introduced to ensure that nobody left the country with Egyptian currency or a range of commodities needed there. A new form was prepared on which people leaving the country were expected to enter those items which might or might not be allowed out. A list of the items was said to be on the back of the form. By some official mischance the backs of the forms were left blank. This error was pointed out to a customs official at Cairo Airport. He examined the form, and then, tongue in cheek, asked, 'Well do you have anything on that list?' 'No!' 'Then put "nothing to declare" on the form.' The joke was not explicit, but it was shared; the problem had been solved pragmatically; bureaucracy was not quite ridiculed, but it was by implication seen to be an ass. The web is not always so easily parted.

82 The northern seated colossi of King Ramesses II at the great temple of Abu Simbel in Nubia. The exterior of this temple has offered welcoming surfaces for visitors to inscribe their names and even accounts of their achievements in this remote district, thus slighting this massive proclamation of royal power.

83 Cairo, early morning, looking from a minaret of the mosque of Er-Rifai towards the Citadel of Saladin (12th century and later) and the mosque of Mohamed Ali, built in the Turkish style (early 19th century).

Commerce and Craftsmanship

Oriental merchants bring to mind strings of camels plodding across the desert, the night stay in a caravanserai, men in long robes and turbans squatting or reclining around a fire, drinking sherbet from delicate glasses or coffee from handleless cups, bales of fine cloth, silks and damasks, spices and incense, exquisitely wrought metal vessels, gold and silver. The Three Kings of Orient are part of the tradition; the tales in the *Arabian Nights*, suitably bowdlerised, fill out the picture; readings of travellers' accounts of journeys in the Levant sharpen the images. Egypt does not quite fit into this picture, but it does have its place securely established there when the status of Cairo in the Islamic world is properly appreciated. Although Egypt was never a country out of bounds to travellers and traders from the West, it was not much visited before the early eighteenth century. The domain of the Ottoman rulers was not very welcoming for infidels, but Turkey itself and the Levantine coastal lands, including Palestine, were essentially points of entry for the merchants of Venice and Genoa, who overcame the mutual antipathies of both sides in order to participate in the lucrative trade which came along the caravan routes from Persia and much further east. Egypt was in a sense marginal to this commercial world, but potentially of prime importance because of its sea links with Arabia, with the Horn of Africa, and ultimately with India. Alexandria, the great invention of the Ptolemies in late antiquity and the point from which the huge cargoes of grain travelled to Italy in Imperial Roman times, had been allowed to crumble and revert to a fishing port of small importance: it is reckoned that its population in

84 The window display of the Camel Jewellery shop near the Bab Zuweila in the heart of medieval Cairo. It is filled with elaborate gold and gold-plated jewellery, still much worn by ordinary Cairene women as marks of status and forms of dowry.

1800 was not more than five thousand. Its fortunes were eventually revived by Mohammed Ali, who caused the Mahmudiya canal to be constructed in 1819, relinking Alexandria with the Nile. Its revitalisation, which continued with increasing pace throughout the nineteenth and the first half of the twentieth centuries, made it into the largest and most important trading port in the eastern Mediterranean after Constantinople. It is strange now to think that when Napoleon invaded Egypt in 1798, the two principal ports were Rosetta and Damietta, the latter being a place much fought over during the wars of the Crusades.

In the years of Alexandria's decline, Cairo was the centre of trade in the country; it was over a hundred miles from the coast, not easy to reach and unwelcoming to foreigners. Nevertheless, determined merchants could, with difficulty, obtain permission to conduct business and to spend time in the small foreign enclaves established both for protection (from the European point of view) and isolation (from the Egyptian point of view). It was rarely the fate of visiting merchants from Europe to suffer more than discomfort, unless they made the mistake of travelling up country. Then they might well meet open hostility; and if not that, then devastating disease. There were also problems over currencies and over methods of trading, and with the penal taxes and dues levied by the rulers of the country and inflated by their corrupt local officials. Matters improved when Egypt became more accessible to European enterprise after the Napoleonic invasion. The floodgates of trade were then opened, and merchants from Italy, France, and Britain, in particular, found the new regime of Mohammed Ali altogether more liberal and conducive to profitable trading in Egypt than in any other eastern Mediterranean country. The regime was, in fact, far from being liberal as far as the population of Egypt was concerned, but from this time up to the revolution in 1952 foreigners enjoyed preferential treatment, which only occasionally brought a blush of shame to their cheeks.

Let us for the moment forget about the major commodities which formed the core of international trade, and consider commerce at a more modest level. Shopping in Egypt is something of an adventure, and one that both fascinates and appals the Western visitor. 'Oh good!', one may say, 'we can bargain.' And so one can, even though there are plenty of shops in Cairo where the price on the object is the price to be paid. Yet, there remain areas of uncertainty, so that the inexperienced visitor may wholly misjudge the local rules by which a transaction is to take place. You do not bargain over a meal in a restaurant or a cup of coffee in a café, but you

85 *above* The Coptic potter Moshen Nossor working on a vase of traditional shape, in a pottery in the village of Garagos near Luxor. Much pottery for general domestic use is still produced in local village workshops.

86 *below* Large water jars (*zias*) and other vessels drying out before being fired in the simple kilns seen in the background: in the village of En-Nazla, near the Masraf el-Wadi in the west Faiyum.

87 *left* A principal room in the Beit es-Suhaimi, one of the few surviving merchant houses of the 17th century in Cairo; it is distinguished by lofty ceilings, rich tile and glass decoration, and elaborate screens and shutters made of turned-wood lattice-work.

88 *above* The distinctive Cairo television tower, viewed through the neon sign of the café Kasr el-Nile on the Gezira Island.

may bargain over the price you pay for a room in a hotel, especially in difficult times or if you plan to stay for more than a few nights. The advantage of securing customers is more important than any *prix fixe*. There is also, even in the shops of the modern city which give all the appearance of being cosmopolitan, often a survival of a way of doing business which belongs to a more leisurely past and the practice of family enterprises. The shopper enters, and approaches a counter where an assistant will deal with her needs. When the transaction is completed, a bill, often in a very simple form, will be made out, and this will be taken by the shopper to the cashier for payment. Here she may meet the owner of the shop or frequently an elderly lady member of the family, possibly the family matriarch, who will take payment and issue the necessary receipt. In turn the receipt is taken to another counter where separate sets of deft fingers will have packed up the purchase. It is all delightfully old-fashioned, labour-intensive and designed to obviate fraud. It is also very time-consuming. You do not pop into such a shop for a quick buy, even if you know exactly what you want and even if you do not have to bargain.

If you make the mistake of trying to bargain in a regular shop in Cairo, or in any other of the principal towns of Egypt, do not be equally mistaken in failing to bargain when the opportunity is presented. No merchant in a bazaar is truly happy at receiving the initial price he names for a product. Bargaining is part of the process of commerce; it should be tough, long drawn out, if possible extended over several days, and always terminated with a sale and satisfaction on both sides. Such a process, of course, is only worth entering into if the prize is worth winning. You do not bargain for a kilo of onions, but you should for a whole crate. It is a nice matter of judgement to know when bargaining is appropriate, and it is probably the case that most short-term visitors to the country should not attempt to acquire the skills beyond what might be needed for the purchase of tourist goods, especially the tawdry modern 'antiquities' which are hawked in the little tourist *suqs* (markets) which preface the entry to many ancient sites. Here you should buy your beads and fancy metalwork, your *galabiyas* and *shibshibs* (slippers), your saddle-bags and leather pouffes, your fly-whisks and headscarves. For such things you can haggle, which is low-grade bargaining, and there will not be too much at stake except your pride. For the real thing, you need to be well prepared, with plenty of time and patience, and brave enough to enter the tempting shops which invite you in the great covered markets of the big towns, but especially in Cairo.

The first impression you receive on entering the *suq* is the lavish presentation of

89 Mohamed Abd el-Sayed Khattab stands in the doorway of his perfumery in the Muski bazaar in Cairo. The elegant flask in his hands characterises his trade, like the decorative jars and glass vessels found in old-fashioned European pharmacies.

90 Keeping the ball rolling. Mechanics work on a well-kept but ancient car - a 1946 Buick Eight - in a back-street behind the Ramses Hilton Hotel in Cairo. Loving care and desperation will keep such a car on the road long after its normal life-span has expired.

the requirements of everyday life - the piles of fresh vegetables and fruit, the large baskets of herbs and spices, the massive bales of brightly dyed cloth, the strings of cheap metal kitchen-ware. And if the *suq* is general and not particular (as so many are in Cairo), you will find between the butchers and the grocers intriguing little shops with select clienteles - the goldsmiths, for example, with a seemingly huge stock of ornaments of all kinds, the components of future bridal dowries, the visible tokens of personal wealth, mostly made in intricate traditional designs and intended chiefly for domestic sales, not for the tourist traffic. There are tiny shops, almost booths, where perfumes and pungent essences (for making up into perfumes) may be purchased, where incense gums in huge crude lumps can be obtained, and, at great price (and therefore suitable for bargaining), pieces of amber, well known for its aphrodisiac properties. In larger *suqs* you may find what can only be seen as the

realisation of one's conception of a sixteenth-century apothecary's shop. Here are the scents and the incense already mentioned, medicinal herbs, dried lizards, unspeakable 'things' bobbing about, all yellow, in ancient jars, roots and infusions, eye of newt, no doubt, and fillet of fenny snake. There may be a small crocodile or large lizard suspended from the ceiling, and, for all one knows - it is Egypt, after all - witches' mummy. Such emporia have little of the modern world in them, apart from the ubiquitous transistor; even the shopkeeper and his assistants seem to take on a medieval demeanour, and in their actions are as slow and deliberate as if they inhabit a world of make-believe.

Most of the business transacted in the bazaars has rather more briskness to it than the arcane manoeuvrings of the establishment for potions and magic. Yet there is in the ancient quarters of Cairo where the old forms of commerce are

91 Sana Ibrahim Girgis prepares dyed wools for the local production of hand-woven tapestries in the village of Garagos near Luxor. The tapestry industry, begun in modern times as an enlightened development near Cairo, has become a flourishing minor industry for the tourist trade.

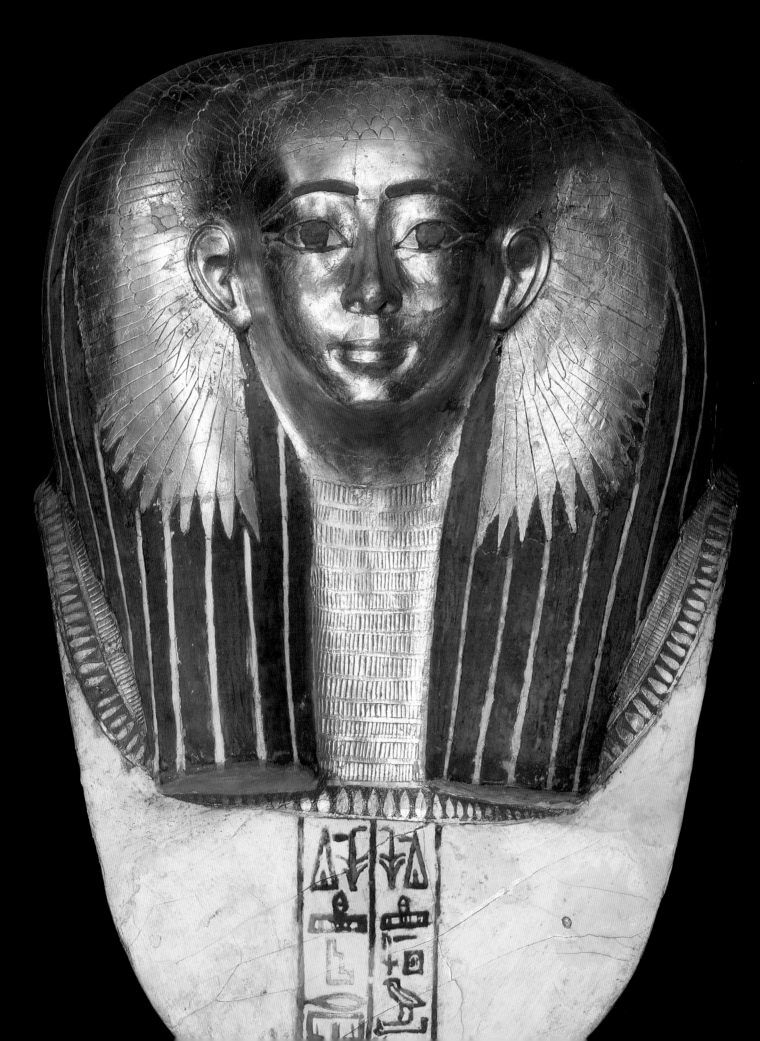

maintained, a timeless quality of pace and spirit which can perhaps be described over-romantically as medieval. The realities of modern international trade have inevitably made their mark elsewhere in the greatest city of the Muslim world. You would not go to the Khan el-Khalili or to the Muski to buy a motor car or a computer, but you would be missing a real experience by going elsewhere for a good carpet or fine metalwork inlaid with intricate designs carried out by time-tested techniques. And there would be a very good chance that what you purchased was made locally or in those places from which such products ought to come. There was a time when everything had its proper source, and proper authenticity. In the middle of the nineteenth century, many cloths came from France, figured muslin (with Paisley patterns) from Scotland, porcelain from Germany; and from Constantinople, as quaintly listed by Lane, 'white slaves, silks, embroidered handkerchiefs and napkins, mouth-pieces for pipes, slippers...'.

Egypt has always been a meeting-place of commercial interests, an entrepôt where the goods of East and West could be traded. It was certainly so in ancient times. Some of the earliest records concern the buying of timber from the Lebanon, the sending of sea-borne expeditions to the land of Punt, somewhere in the Horn of Africa, to bring back the exotic products of equatorial regions - animal skins, ivory, ebony, incense. These last products could also be brought across the desert routes south of Egypt, although these were open to hostile attacks in Nubia; they could even be imported illegally, escaping the customs posts at the fortresses of Lower Nubia. One of the most charming and specific events depicted in a tomb shows the arrival of a party of Asiatics, sometimes described as bedouin, in the Oryx nome of Middle Egypt while Khnumhotpe was the regional governor in the reign of King Ammenemes II of the Twelfth Dynasty (c. 1929-1892 BC). The little group, on foot and with pack donkeys, brings eye-paint from Sinai; they are traders, or just pedlars - who can now tell? By such small groups, no doubt, much of the minor traffic was carried on. Ships brought the commodities from the Levant, from Cyprus and from Crete, and later from the Greek islands. There was oil and wine, as well as timber, silver and copper; rare lapis-lazuli which somehow passed along the caravan routes of Central Asia from Afghanistan, its only known ancient source. Trade and commerce flourish best through the initiatives of individuals, seeking and meeting the special needs of the people they service. By royal interference traders could be helped or hindered, and by royal patronage trade could expand. Gold from Egypt was the most valued of exports to Western Asia, and manufactured goods of fine

92 Painted and gilded mummy-mask of Middle Kingdom date (c.1900 BC): a minor masterpiece in the simple medium of cartonnage, a kind of ancient papier-mâché, made of layers of linen and plaster, and then moulded. The vulture headdress suggests that the owner was a princess (British Museum, 29770).

workmanship were highly prized in ancient Babylon. Tomb-scenes show boats arriving in port and unloading goods of various kinds, probably cargoes from Syria or even from the north of Egypt, sent up to Thebes.

Some tombs also contain fascinating glimpses of the precursors of the present-day market stalls - little booths set up on the quayside selling all kinds of produce and fast food and drink to the crew members from the boats. A rather detailed series of scenes in a Fifth-Dynasty tomb at Saqqara shows even more of the marketing processes of the mid-third millennium BC. Bargaining is certainly going on, and from what is known of buying and selling in ancient Egypt, bargaining was very much the essential procedure. Transactions carried out by means of a stable currency are relatively easy to manage; valuations of commodities can be established in the market-place; exchange rates between different currencies fixed by the balances and checks of the market. In a monetary system, if there is to be bargaining, at least there is a common standard against which value can be gauged. But if there is no coinage, then to find the value of any item must be a matter of very fine negotiation. It is known that at most periods certain basic commodities had established values in terms of each other; thus, in the early Middle Kingdom the value of barley against emmer-wheat was in the ratio of three to two. Knowing this value, it would be possible to estimate other valuations according to local standards for other commodities, and even for individual items of everyday use. If you wanted to acquire a bed, made by a carpenter, you would have to arrive at a price by agreement, i.e. by bargaining; this might mean putting up a series of objects to make up the value of the bed - a few pots, a little oil, a pair of sandals, a stool, a length of cloth - all together being enough to satisfy the seller.

Such a system seems hopelessly clumsy and open to all kinds of abuse; but it lasted for thousands of years, and a very advanced economy was so managed without recorded difficulty. If you do not have money, and you do not know money, you do not miss money. You use the existing procedures accordingly. It must be supposed that in the small transactions which represented the extent of most people's experience with commerce, both buyers and sellers were willing performers and therefore usually ready to conclude a bargain to the satisfaction of all sides. A problem in setting out to conduct business was the availability of suitable things to use. A farmer would have the surplus of crops from his land before it was removed for taxes by the local agents. A labourer or official would be paid in kind, and, if employed by an institution, probably in the form of food rations - quantities of

93 *above* A scene of jewellery-makers from the tomb of Sobkhotpe at Thebes (Eighteenth Dynasty, c.1375 BC). They sit on three- and four-legged stools, and some drill beads with bow drills, just as may be seen in the bazaars of Cairo to the present day (British Museum, 920).

94 *below* Small industries like the brush-making factory shown here help to establish the economy of new developments like that of Ashara Ramadan in the desert east of Cairo.

grain, for example - and usually more than would be needed to feed him and his family; again, the surplus would represent his liquid cash. The employees of temples were able to participate in the reversion of offerings, again receiving portions which would not only support families but provide something extra for that rainy day, which in Egypt would certainly have been very occasional and unexpected.

Although money began to creep into the Egyptian economy towards the end of the Pharaonic period in the fourth century BC, it did not become an essential ingredient in the trading practices of the country until the Ptolemies introduced and encouraged the commercial enterprises that had made the Greeks such successful traders throughout the Mediterranean world. The advantages of using cash instead of kind were quickly appreciated in Egypt, and the adjustment to a monetary system seems to have been made with singularly little difficulty. There were, however, problems over metal content, as most of the silver for everyday coinage had to be imported. For much of the Roman Period, up to the end of the third century AD, it was forbidden to export coins minted in the country. It was an early taste of what was to happen again in the aftermath of the modern revolution, when very tight controls were imposed on currency (but then in the form of banknotes). In other respects the Egyptian economy remained in good balance up until late antiquity, due principally to the exceptionally stable and successful agricultural system. The potential ability to farm intensively and to produce substantial surpluses was greatly exploited during the Ptolemaic and Roman Periods, when large estates were developed and the movement of exports was facilitated by the use of internationally accepted currency. Royal and private banks, chiefly set up for fiscal purposes, also provided the financial basis for a strong exporting economy. Many of these advantages, new to the native Egyptian economy, were readily understood by the Egyptians, who profited from the general prosperity. Sadly, the system did not survive the Islamic conquest, and a slow decline overtook agriculture over the centuries until it was revived in the nineteenth century. Its present success in the competitive world of food production is seriously diminished by the needs of a rapidly increasing population, as has already been pointed out. Yet, the diligent shopper in London may from time to time find Egyptian produce on the shelves of supermarkets; and special delight comes from finding supplies of delicious Egyptian potatoes, still (and preferably) carrying traces of that Egyptian earth - Nile mud - on which so much of Egypt's life and prosperity has depended. Agriculture, however, is not enough to sustain the modern Egyptian economy, and industry, from the

95 The southern end of the Suez Canal. Seen from a minaret of the Badir mosque in Port Taufiq, an eastern-bound convoy moves out of the canal into deep water. The canal, through its tolls, is still Egypt's greatest earner of foreign currency.

production of oil and the products of oil to the manufacture of cars and trucks, has been developed in ways that could scarcely have been imagined at the time of the revolution.

In their own way Egyptians have whole-heartedly embraced their particular industrial revolution, and have brought to it an element of local small-scale activity which at times gives it the impression of being almost a cottage enterprise. Indeed, the ancient craft techniques, which are as readily displayed in the specialist shops and booths of the bazaars as in the vitrines of museums, seem to have been adapted to handle the care of the proliferating machines and gadgets of life which are found throughout the country, often obtained abroad by the armies of Egyptians who have worked in other, richer, Arab states for substantially greater wages than they could obtain in Egypt. The introduction to modern machines and their maintenance came through the motor car, and the evidence of the skill and diligence of the Egyptian mechanic are demonstrated through the large numbers of old cars still kept on the road in spite of the punishing treatment which they receive from drivers who regard their performance as a gladiatorial exercise. Model T Fords, in particular, seemed to monopolise the taxi population of the towns of Middle Egypt up until the early 1970s; dowager-looking Rolls-Royces may still be seen crawling through the traffic-clogged streets of Cairo or speeding out of town to the Delta to some diminished old estate. The mechanics who work in the untidy garages that disfigure most towns, and even villages in the countryside, are masters at keeping on the road vehicles which elsewhere would be thought to be well past their throw-away dates. Not knowing much about the technicalities of the machines they work on, they are inspired by the instincts of a preserving society, and are virtuosi of the wire and insulating tape tradition. One must admire the fantasy that will encourage a workman to attempt to be a craftsman, and to try, metaphorically (for Egypt is primarily a Muslim country), to make a silk purse from a sow's ear. It is often the lack of good materials that obliges a man to make, for example, a suitcase that looks like leather but turns out to be of cardboard. Egyptians can be very skilled bodgers. Given the chance, they can also be excellent craftsmen.

The walk we have just taken through the bazaar will have revealed not only the products of the skilled craftsman but also the practice of the skills of the very craftsmen themselves. In a corner near a jeweller's shop you may find a man squatting, working a primitive lathe or a bow-drill, shaping, polishing and piercing the pretty pebbles found in such plenty in the Eastern Desert. Stone-working on a large or small scale has been an Egyptian craft for five thousand years or more. Jewellery surviving from earliest antiquity shows the first exercises in the lapidary's skills. The great buildings, beginning from the time of the Step Pyramid, reveal a remarkable capacity to quarry, shape and build with soft and hard stones. Nothing seems to have defeated the ancient Egyptian craftsman, although he never tackled the truly hard stones, the real gems, possibly because they had not yet been isolated and identified for their potential beauty. To work the next grade, the semi-precious stones, carnelian, amethyst, garnet, turquoise, agates, and to produce, in addition to beads, small figures, inlays and many kinds of cosmetic and other trinkets, needed great care and much skill. The shaping was done almost entirely by grinding and drilling, sand being used as the principal cutting tool. But the great joy of ancient jewellery and its allied arts was the extraordinary sense of design and taste that informs so much of what was produced. In fitting tiny inlays into gold settings (cloisons), with intricate techniques of brazing, soldering, granulation, wire-making (though not, apparently, wire-drawing) - almost the whole range that a modern jeweller would use - stunning pieces were produced, of kinds that would be difficult to reproduce today.

The jewellers of the Cairo bazaars can still dazzle with lavish displays of gold ornaments: very pretty small necklaces and earrings can be found, and among the most attractive items are simple strings of beads of matching and contrasting semi-precious stones. Unfortunately, the tendency towards heaviness and opulence in design - a result partly of considering a piece of jewellery more as an investment than a work of art - renders much of what is on offer unacceptable to Western taste. But the skills are there, just as they were in antiquity and as they flourished in the centuries between. A fluctuation in taste from light to heavy can be detected in the development of design, from the exquisite pectoral pendants and filigree work of the Middle Kingdom to the somewhat coarser (though technically masterful) work exemplified by the jewellery found on the body of King Tutankhamun, and from the less well-known but astonishingly accomplished splendour of the bulky trinkets retrieved from the royal tombs of the Twenty-First and Twenty-Second Dynasties at Tanis to the fine and lightly designed work of classical times, degenerating to the somewhat tawdry but pretentious pieces of late antiquity under Byzantine influence. After the Islamic invasion, design and purpose in jewellery were hugely influenced by Arab tradition and Muslim requirements; new techniques of metal-working were introduced into the ateliers of Egyptian goldsmiths and jewellers; silver was more widely exploited, and filigree became popular. But still the craftsman squatted on the ground or sat on a little stool, just as he can be seen at work in the private tombs of the New Kingdom at Thebes.

In other scenes in these same tombs you can see the practice of other crafts which today form the standard repertoire of production for the bazaar. The beating of metal sheet to raise vessels seems to have changed little since ancient times. Pottery is still produced on primitive wheels, although not in the neighbourhood of the bazaar. The glass industry of antiquity, which in Egypt reached its peak in the late Eighteenth Dynasty, revived in the Roman Period but then showed little of the distinctive Egyptian flair for colour and design. The very simple basic shapes which became common throughout the Roman world were developed and modified back into native styles in medieval Egypt, and some of that tradition can still be seen in the attractive blue, green and purple flasks, bowls and drinking glasses, which are so fragile to carry in one's luggage and which are made, so it is said, mostly from recycled lemonade bottles.

Among the most striking survivals from ancient Egypt are chairs, thrones, boxes, beds, chests and other pieces of furniture. They display all the skills and techniques of good joinery and cabinet-making. The structure of pieces is amazingly sound by modern standards: joints are varied and accurately cut; fine woods are exploited with an eye to their graining; soft woods are 'disguised' with fine veneers and embellished with inlays of ivory, precious metals, coloured stones and faience; intricate marquetry was practised; chests were painted as brilliantly as any Italian marriage coffer. For a country that had almost no good timber, imports supplied the deficiency, and the native craftsman excelled in exploiting the wide variety of what was obtained from northern and southern lands. Remarkably dry conditions and extraordinary good luck have ensured the survival of more good examples than should ever have been expected. Your walk through the bazaar will show that the tradition of joiner has survived, and that hand-made furniture is still being produced in the carpenters' shops of most large towns. You do not have to sit long in a café overlooking a busy street before you see a donkey-cart pass by piled high with elaborate furniture - usually in the style of the Second Empire or even earlier. Both the great Napoleon and Napoleon III, through his wife the Empress Eugénie, left their mark on taste in the decorative arts in Egypt, and this persists even today. Scarlet upholstery, carved and gilded ornament proliferate on the popular, but uncomfortable, salon pieces that remain in fashion in the houses of minor executives and civil servants.

96 The carpenter Ahmed Mohamed works on a chair in the street outside the joiner's workshop in Sharia Rahib, close to the Bab el-Khalq and the Islamic Museum in Cairo. The demand for elaborately carved and upholstered furniture is still met by modern woodworkers exercising old techniques.

Step into one of the workshops - probably run by Copts, for most carpenters and cabinet-makers are Christian - and you will see the young apprentices carving designs on chair-backs from old pattern books, using a wide variety of old chisels and gouges and working almost entirely by eye. It is undeniable that the skills remain, even if one could wish that they were put to better use.

The story can be repeated for many other crafts, for metal-working and leather-working in particular; and the spirit of craftsmanship, at a lower level perhaps, can be found in the huge variety of maintenance services exploiting useful artisan skills. Egypt is a country where it is still possible to get a small job done, a repair carried out, a service effected, quickly, willingly, and without having to pay a huge premium for calling someone to one's home. Often willingness outstrips capability, especially where no previous expert knowledge has existed. There was enterprise, no doubt, behind a notice in the smart suburb of Zamalek: 'English plumber available'. Such initiative, backed by proper skills and an understanding of modern bathroom fittings, could, however, only succeed if the specialist also understood the need to satisfy the demands of his clients with the expedition of the local workman, who would not question the most unreasonable and unsocial demands for service. Further, any Egyptian plumber's mate he might recruit would soon pick up enough in the way of practical knowledge to start up on his own, and breed a new generation of 'English' plumbers.

The interplay of ideas and techniques which follows naturally from the contacts between nations was at work as much in antiquity as it is today. And in antiquity Egypt played a most important part in the formulation and exploitation of new ideas. For the best part of two thousand years, Egypt, although open to foreign influences and imports, was politically very stable, and this stability resulted in a settled society in which much could develop and mature without interruption through war or racial movements. It is rarely possible to establish priority where skills and technical processes are concerned. In the favourable conditions of Egypt, so much evidence has survived in the form of actual objects which can illustrate the practical application of craft processes and artistic techniques; it is not very profitable to try to pin down precisely what the sources were in every case. There has been a tendency in the past to seek the origins of innovations elsewhere; but in the end what matters is not priority but achievement.

97 *opposite* **Bab Zuweila, one of the surviving gates in the Fatimid walls of Cairo, dating from the 11th century. This view is taken from the steps of the 15th-century mosque of Sultan Muayyad Sheikh, one of Barquq's mamelukes.**

98 *overleaf* **The corniche in Alexandria, from the famous Cecil Hotel. Alexandria was rebuilt and revived as the greatest eastern Mediterranean port in the mid-19th century.**

A Gentle People

Walking about the narrow streets and covered bazaars of Cairo or any other city in Egypt is a special experience. For the inexperienced visitor there is much that is original, strange, even disturbing. There may be no motor vehicles, but you may easily be surprised by a donkey or a donkey-cart, even by a camel padding quietly up behind you: the shout of his driver will mean nothing to you; you should sense when to step aside, and you should certainly not expect an animal to give way to you. The people too are different; they will mostly be men, walking purposefully with grace and dignity or collecting in small groups to gossip, then withdrawing by preference to the nearest café. Many will still wear traditional clothes, headcloths or turbans and *galabiyas*, the first wonderfully white and carefully turned round the head, the latter in sombre colours with perhaps a little tasteful embroidery at the neck. So dressed they look more properly at home in their surroundings than those who are wearing suits. The red *tarbush* is now rarely seen, although up until the revolution it was commonly worn by many, including government servants, both Egyptian and European. There will be women about also, many in the traditional black which has all to do with status and nothing to do with mourning. Some will wear Western clothes, the common dress of most Egyptian women in society, business and the professions, but many now affect headscarves and other articles of dress partially to hide the face. The traditional veil, still commonly worn by bedouin women and in very fundamentalist circles, is rarely seen; but the traditional modesty is still observed by village women, who will draw their headcloth over the

99 Guardian in the principal room of the Beit es-Suhaimi, a 17th-century merchant's house in Cairo. The intricate *meshrabiya* (turned-wood screens) enabled ladies to observe what was going on in the court below, without being visible themselves.

lower part of the face in the presence of male strangers. Generally speaking, even today, etiquette does not allow a man to address a woman directly in the casual circumstances of the street; the reaction is likely to be one of acute embarrassment, or, if there are several women together, a torrent of disconcerting laughter.

There is more that is strange. On the whole, although you may be solicited to buy by the touts that lurk in most shop doorways, with the engaging cry of 'No charge for looking', you will be allowed to pass along without hindrance. That at least is reassuring. But if you want to remain unbothered, walk with determination, even if you are not quite sure where you are going. Hesitation may lead to your being accosted, usually by a well-meaning young man eager to try out his English and truly to be helpful. Sadly, the impression may be given that the intention is to take you somewhere, to make you buy something you do not want, or take part in some improper activity. It is usually not so, but how do you judge intention when everything is so strange, and the umbilical cord attaching you to your tour guide may be momentarily severed? The solution is for you to discover. The best advice is not to allow yourself to be pressured, to be firm in your intentions, and if you find yourself in despair, climb into the nearest taxi (there is nearly always one handy) and retreat. In normal situations you should never feel afraid, because you will in fact be surrounded by some of the friendliest people in the world, whose curiosity will be real interest and whose readiness to help will be a proper expression of the natural hospitality of the country. Even so, you may not be able to avoid feeling a little uncomfortable in such a strange environment, the strangeness of which is heightened by unusual sounds and smells.

Sound, or rather noise, is ever-present in the towns of Egypt, wherever people gather. It soon becomes evident that noise is the acceptable background to outdoor life, even in houses where a boisterous family life goes on. Egyptians seem incapable of talking quietly to each other, and when gossip is intense or argument heated, then the exchanges become louder and louder, and to one who is unable to judge what is going on it may seem that the time for exchanging blows has come. The sounds of workmen issuing from a warren of shops and improvised manufactories, the hammering of metal, the roar of small furnaces, the hum of lathes and clatter of looms; and above and behind all, the relentless accompaniment of music churned out by a myriad of radios. The music itself is seemingly endless and seamless, played mostly by large string bands, with singers worrying the themes of popular song, which are here rather more decorous than in the West; the cadences

100 *above* A double wedding in the ballroom of the Nile Hilton Hotel, Cairo. It has become customary for fine weddings to be celebrated with much ceremony, display and music in the most fashionable hotels in the city.

101 *below* Conjugal affection in the Old Kingdom (c.2400 BC). A painted limestone pair-statue of the high official Katep and his wife Hetepheres with her arm around his waist. Unusually, both are shown at the same height (British Museum, 1181).

are strange, the harmonies distinctly oriental, but the general effect is somewhat homogenised and can be exhausting to the untutored listener. Momentarily evocative, even nostalgic, especially if heard by chance away from the country, a little more of such music can soon be enough. And over all, cries, shouts, voices raised in anger, in persuasion, in argument, or just simply in loud conversation.

As for smells, things have changed a little in the last thirty years. Ever since the advent of the internal combustion engine there has been a strong smell of petrol in the streets of Egyptian towns. Petrol is cheap and is used for all kinds of cleaning purposes; it is splashed about with rare abandon, and in the hot atmosphere evaporates more readily than in cold climates. Its smell is pervasive, subtly blended with the pungent presence of donkey and camel urine - the last less evident today than formerly. Rather more delicious smells come from the little stands and barrows that sell the Egyptian equivalent of 'food on the hoof' and from the tempting fruit shops open to the street; while, in the relative seclusion of back streets, the smoke of charcoal braziers and of incense gives the air a special quality.

A thing that strikes the observant visitor as he walks about an Egyptian town is the apparent lack of pressures in daily life. There may be bustle, but not rush. There are always plenty of people about doing nothing much. They are not, it seems, unemployed, they do not look deprived or miserable, although, of course, there are in a great city like Cairo many people who are in dire circumstances. But here we are considering the many who have any amount of time to stand about chatting and sit in the cafés which play such a prominent part in the daily routine of many men. The practice of taking it easy is developed into a fine art here, and many Egyptians are very competent practitioners. Many seem even to have succeeded in incorporating times of leisure into the stringent ways of modern business and professional life. Café life goes on all day, and to the detached observer may seem to be rather dull. The little marble-topped tables and rather rickety caned chairs, which seem obligatory, are all somewhat reminiscent of an old-fashioned *salon de thé*; they stand in severe rows, often open to the street and designed in their arrangement for wandering in and out. The patrons are almost without exception male, even in these days of greater feminine freedom; many will be elderly, well wrapped up against the cold until the overcoat becomes unbearable in the heat; a few real old-timers will wear the *tarbush*. They sit singly or in pairs, rarely in larger gatherings, reading papers, drinking coffee, or more commonly tea, very sweet and in glasses; if there is talk it will be loud, as we have already mentioned. Some will come for a smoke,

102 Fatma and her mother Towhida in traditional costume beside their house in the village of Ezbet Bashendi in the oasis of El-Kharga. They do not wear the veil, but Fatma displays characteristic dowry jewellery in the form of coins.

using the traditional oriental pipes, most noticeably the *nargila* or hubble-bubble, the water-pipe; regulars may have their own pipe specially kept for them, while others will just bring their own mouth-piece, which can be something very personal and special, perhaps made of amber. This one may have arranged to play cards with a friend, or chess (not so common now); another pair may engage in what always seems to be a gladiatorial contest of trictrac, a form of backgammon in which the pieces are slammed hard on the board to the accompaniment of much excited shouting. There may also be the importunities of street vendors, selling not so much the carpets of years ago but dark glasses, cigarettes, lottery tickets; shoe-cleaners will be welcomed, with their little portable equipments and deft movements punctuated by the ringing of a bell which means 'change feet!'. It always seems to be a real act of supererogation in Egypt's dusty land, to have one's shoes cleaned several times a day; but, apart from the good service one does one's shoes, there is also an element of charity in employing the often wretched boot-black.

The exercise of charity is deeply part of the Islamic ethic, and accepted in small and large ways by devout Muslims, and also by most people in Egypt whatever faith they ascribe to or even practise. The shelling out of small change is one matter that upsets many visitors; the constant demands for *baksheesh* are intolerable, and some people become so obsessed with avoiding the giving of negligible sums that they can scarcely enjoy any activity that involves a modest service requiring modest reward. A moment's thought about the actual cost of the charitable distribution in an average day should restore equanimity; but there is always the problem of having the appropriate coin in pocket or purse. You cannot decently ask for change if you are disbursing trivial largesse, although it would not be thought so odd by the practically minded potential recipient. The charitable Egyptian, however, always seems to have the right coin available, and whether in a café, in parking his car, in leaving a mosque or a church, where beggars are ever present, can produce the suitable gratuity, hoped for though not demanded. It is not difficult to do it, it is not crippling if it is done sensibly, it is good for one's own spirit, and it is not demeaning for either side. You should never do anything, say anything, or engage in any activity which may indicate a lack of respect for a person's integrity and personal pride.

There is, in fact, no surer way of ruining a promising enterprise in Egypt than by neglecting the dignity of the other party. It can easily be done through the exercise of arbitrary decisions without proper consideration of other points of view, by imputing impropriety or lack of nerve. The Egyptian is not by nature a bombast, a bully, noticeably brave, or one to drag his coat; but he can be roused to unreasonable fury if the wrong thing is said or done. The male virtues and associated prowess are mightily important; equally so are the traditional female virtues. In a marriage you cannot impugn the former without slandering the latter. In such matters never speak lightly, or you will rue it. In village life, many of the nastiest scandals end up with the wielding of the lethal *turiya*, a cross between hoe and spade, an immensely handy tool for digging, clearing earth, and splitting skulls. The lawless acts that are so much the subjects of gossip in the countryside seem mostly to be the result of personal, often family, quarrels, in which indeed honour and pride may be involved. In town ordinary lawlessness is remarkably well contained. It would be foolish to pretend that 'things' don't happen in the towns, but one is far less aware of crime than anywhere in the West. The hot-headed squabble that may end in a broken head, a bloody nose or even a stabbing is usually unpremeditated, and the result often of some trivial encounter or accident. For the rest, even Cairo is unusually free from street crime: a bag may be snatched, but it is rare to hear of muggings, and the elderly have the protection of the deeply ingrained respect for age which has all but disappeared in European and American life.

At the other end of the scale, children also escape the outrageous behaviour that has diminished societies elsewhere so severely in modern times. Children in Egypt tend to be over-indulged, cossetted and spoilt beyond reason, as visitors may infer from the knowing way in which the young behave. Babies have always been precious in Egypt, especially as infant mortality used to be such a major problem; so they too are almost excessively protected from the hazards of life. If you ever want to know what swaddling clothes are, glance into an Egyptian pram in the town, or into the quaint mud cradle supports found in the courts of village houses, designed to keep a babe out of reach of snakes and scorpions; you will see the little dear so wrapped, confined, trapped, by clothes and coverlets, mostly of wool no matter the weather, that any germ can only attack through the most vulnerable points which are exposed - the eyes, the nose, the ears and the mouth - the very parts which in the ancient rituals were 'opened' so that the mummy could function properly after burial. This care and protection lavished on the very young continues until late childhood in most families. Children, after all, have always been the most important resource available to the poor man in Egypt; to have many children should mean that a fair number may survive to adulthood. So, the strongly knit family

remains of first importance in Egypt today, providing personal and national bases for stability. Few Egyptians are happier than when they are with their families, and the respect and affection generated in a family ensures a continuity of the kind of careful concern for the old and for the sick which is so rapidly disappearing in most Western countries.

This respect may serve as a strong and distinct thread of continuity that can be traced back through the generations to the accepted modes of conduct approved in the ancient world. It has often been pointed out that religion in ancient Egypt, as it comes to us from the massive textual legacy of royal and private tombs and of papyri, is rather thin in ethical or moral content. The principal purpose of prayer and worship was to honour the deity. But it would be wrong to think that the observance of the religious forms did not imply also suitable standards of behaviour. What was expected of a person to live an acceptably good life is incorporated in the list of activities and attitudes implicitly contained in what is usually called the Negative Confession. It represents a kind of passing-out examination to which a dead person was subjected before he was allowed entry to the realm of Osiris; it forms an invariable part of the selection of spells of the *Book of the Dead* buried with the deceased. Here, by denying that he has performed certain kinds of activity during his life, the subject exposes the acceptable modes of behaviour in ancient Egypt, and these are replete with moral implications: 'I have not told lies', 'I have not terrorised', 'I have not been angry', 'I have not robbed', 'I have not killed men', 'I have not gossiped', 'I have not ignored the truth'. There is much else, for there were forty-two individual items to deny, but some of them apply only in explicitly ancient Egyptian contexts, such as 'I have not killed a sacred bull'. To live one's mortal span according to these principles - for principles they are - would strain the determination of the most morally devoted of people, and one should not suppose that in their ordinary daily activities the ancient Egyptians were particularly better behaved than most. Nevertheless, there is evidence that they formed a pretty passive population, not much given to the worst excesses of behaviour characteristic in antiquity among those peoples and tribes which glorified war, saluted the strong, admired the man of hard decision.

This last appreciation may not accord well with the common image of the king smiting his enemies, trampling the foreigner underfoot, brave in battle, supported by Monthu the warrior god and by Amon-Re, King of the Gods. But the king was himself a god, and his behaviour was not the behaviour expected from his peoples.

103 The countryman Bayoumi Ibrahim by the door of his house near Tamia. He radiates the confidence of a successful modern farmer, whose experience is rooted over many generations in the fertile soil of the Faiyum.

104 Two male guests at the funeral feast (perpetuated for eternity) of the vizier Ramose in his tomb in Thebes (reigns of Amenophis III-IV, c. 1355-1350 BC). These serene officials reflect the success of an unparalleled period of relative peace and prosperity.

They were seen to be subservient, mild, carrying out their duties and services on behalf of the king, and earning merit not by behaving violently but by acting justly and scrupulously, treating the interests of ordinary people as if they were their own. The ideal subject was one who had responsibilities and exercised them punctiliously and without favouritism. Again we can turn to texts to learn what was expected. The compositions that make up what is called 'wisdom literature' dwell at length on the proper ways in which one should behave. Parents should look after their children, see that they are properly fed and educated, and that they are so nurtured that they grow up honouring their parents, properly appreciating all that has been done on their behalf. But if a child ignores his training and behaves badly, he should be suitably punished, both for his own good and as a lesson for others. The poor should always be treated with compassion and defended against those who may seek to exploit them; they should be fed and clothed and helped along the way. Towards equals one should act in moderation, never boasting or seeking

to get the upper hand. To one's superiors one should behave with proper deference, acknowledging their seniority and authority and carrying out their orders with expedition and without complaint.

The moral tone of all these 'Instructions', 'Admonitions', 'Teachings', is overwhelming in its propriety. The authors, usually said to have been famous sages, even historical figures like the vizier Ptahhotep, could, without great adaptations, have achieved success in the field of Victorian improving literature. Did Egyptians ever manage to act as the books recommended? The ideal presumably mirrors to some extent the actuality; so a moderate benefit of the doubt could probably be allowed. In a sense it all came down in the end to the proper ordering of the world according to the divine principle manifested in the form of the goddess Ma'at. She, the embodiment of order, and seen as the divine personification of Truth, was the arbiter of balance in the world. In the ancient world such a divine conception could perhaps only have been evolved in Egypt. Egypt was an unusually stable

105 In the harbour of Rashid. Behind the two girls on the boat is the fort where the Rosetta Stone, key to the decipherment of hieroglyphs, was found.

106 *left* A game of dominoes in the El-Shams café near the Courts of Justice in Cairo; a few solitary individuals content themselves with water-pipes (*nargilas*).

107 *above* In the tomb of the scribe Nakhte in the Theban Necropolis, a group of ladies join in the entertainment of the funerary feast; one hands a mandrake fruit to another (Eighteenth Dynasty, c.1400 BC).

country, not subject to regular invasion and violent political change as were most Near-Eastern countries. It was the only country of accepted fixed limits in a world of changing boundaries. From the earliest times when a single unified land was achieved, until the end of the Pharaonic period - almost three thousand years in all - Upper and Lower Egypt were established with quite precisely defined boundaries to the north, the east and the south. The Mediterranean Sea, the Red Sea and the first Nile cataract marked the limits of Egypt proper; to the west the line of the desert oases provided a slightly less precise limit. A clearly defined land, for the most part able to maintain a tranquil society, was a place where a very settled culture could develop, where people could readily appreciate the advantages of peace and order.

Certain other literary compositions, allied in tone to the more specifically moral wisdom literature, lay emphasis on the troubles that overtook Egypt at times when order did break down and when foreigners were able to upset the level progress of life in the country. At such times, particularly in those periods called Intermediate by Egyptologists, the balancing influence of Ma'at failed and disorder followed, shown not only in political matters but also in the management of land and the control of the flood and of irrigation generally. The efficient ordering of the water supply especially affected the lives of ordinary people, and brought home to them the advantages of the usual, well-controlled regime. The burden of so much ancient writing is this settled order; there is no vaunting of the military life, for example. It would be foolish to think that life in Egypt during the long stretches of peace and stability was a bed of roses for all. The difficult lives of the many engaged in hard manual toil has already been touched on, and it is not difficult to imagine that in the countryside the pressures of weather, officialdom and personal tragedy rendered the lives of most people uncertain and painful. Nevertheless, the laborious existences of people are more easily endured when the general situation in a country is stable than when life is threatened by the possibility of serious invasion or of periodic incursions by marauding bands of pillaging foreigners. The cry of the ancient Egyptian could well have been 'Please, leave me along; I know I cannot avoid the problems of the landlord, the tax-gatherer, the flood and the locust; but otherwise, give me the quiet life.'

The Arcadian picture provided by the vignettes of country and social life found in tombs was intended to create the right environment for a happy posthumous existence for the tomb-owner: the crops grow tall, the cattle flourish, everyone at the party looks well and enjoys the hospitality on offer. Occasionally a hint of trouble suggests that even in Elysium all might not always run smoothly. The back-chat between the supporting characters in tomb-scenes can be very informative: workmen by their asides indicate that it does not do to go easy on the job; gossiping is not popular with the boss; the stick may be wielded by officers; girls may quarrel in the fields and pull each other's hair; a lady may overdo her drinking at the feast and suffer the inevitable consequences; cattle may fall foul of crocodiles; new-born calves may be snatched by jackals. But in the best circumstances the minor troubles of life will take their place in the general order of things, and do no more than emphasise the advantages of what is normal; the exception does here prove the rule.

What does happen, however, if matters become difficult even without any intervention from outside Egypt's borders? What if internal order crumbles and the regularity of life is threatened from within? Then, under unusual pressures, the people may grumble, hold demonstrations, join in rioting and ultimately in revolution. Politics and religion were the most likely causes of trouble, as indeed they have so often been elsewhere at all periods. The references in ancient texts to periods when law and order broke down are not sufficiently explicit to enable the historian to determine either the nature or the extent of any civil disorder. The misery which seems to have been widespread in Egypt during the First Intermediate Period (*c.* 2134-2040 BC) apparently started with political disintegration, and then was made much worse by a series of low Niles, drought and famine, leading to the incursion of desert tribes seeking the better chances of survival in Egypt, deficient though the country was under the circumstances. The general discontent demanded a political solution, which in time was provided by the rulers of the southern Theban Eleventh Dynasty; the reunion of the whole land brought back order (Ma'at), and the better, even prosperous times of the Twelfth Dynasty ensued. There is not much evidence that throughout this troublous time civil disorder in the form of rioting took place. During the worrying period in the Twentieth Dynasty when Egypt was again under considerable pressures from outside, the running of the country suffered, and there survive good records of the strikes organised by the workmen of the royal tombs, complaining about the non-provision of their rations and other supplies. These were scarcely nation-shaking events, but we are in no position to say what may have been happening elsewhere in the country.

In more recent times the gradual political awakening of Egypt during the early

decades of the twentieth century led to many periods of civil disturbance, occasions of rioting and demonstrations, particularly by students. The burning of much of the business centre of Cairo in January 1952 was ostensibly sparked off by the killing of auxiliary police in a confrontation with British troops in the Canal Zone, but it may have been more deliberately provoked by political agitators. By international standards this riot was inconsiderable, but it had a momentous influence on Egyptian thinking and was the cause of remarkable national shame. Its violence and considerable loss of life should be contrasted with what happened just six months later when the revolution toppled King Farouk. It has been said that this event was marked by 'the good temper and lack of vindictiveness' of the leaders of the revolution. Success was achieved without bloodshed, and the subsequent treatment of those who might have been considered suitable subjects for the guillotine in an earlier event of similar kind was remarkably humane.

The worse cases of civil unrest on a fairly regular basis are recorded in Alexandria, from the time of its foundation until the late Roman Period. The city was populated by an extraordinary mixture of races, and the tensions that developed fired political and religious disturbances. A late third-century revolt which elevated a political unknown, Lucius Domitius Domitianus, to the position of emperor was violently put down after months of insurgence, and the legitimate emperor Diocletian, whose name elicited reasonable fury among Egyptian Christians for centuries thereafter, vowed bloody revenge on the city. He threatened to continue the slaughter of its inhabitants until the blood reached his horse's knees. Providentially, his horse stumbled as he entered the city and the threat retreated; the grateful citizens put up a statue of the horse. This particular revolt was distinct from the endemic trouble which affected the city. The Alexandrian mob was notorious for its violence and viciousness, its fickleness and its unpredictability. The large Jewish community was constantly the subject of communal violence; the Copts were regularly divided among themselves over the theological disputes which marked the early centuries of Christian debate in the eastern Mediterranean world; Christians and pagans were regularly at each other's throats. The Greeks, seeing themselves as the heirs of Alexander and the natural torch-bearers of civilisation, were never averse from persecuting those who thought differently. They were not averse either from playing on the prejudices of the urban rabble. In the Byzantine Period, the troubles often centred on the chariot races in the hippodrome. Partisanship was vigorous and as disruptive as the allegiances to football clubs today. The leading

108 Three generations of a Faiyum farming family stand in front of a waterwheel by the Bahr Sinnuris just north of Medinet el-Faiyum: Ropey Goda on the left, Bedawi Selim (his son-in-law) on the right, and young grandson Ashraf Bedawi Selim in front.

charioteers were public figures with gangs of mindless supporters, whose devotion to one or another star could be harnessed to political ends. The partisan passions of the hippodrome were in Egypt special to Alexandria. Today soccer violence is not unknown in Egypt, for the game is supported there with as much devotion as anywhere; but such scenes as disfigure sporting life in other countries are only seen in Egypt when the game is particularly crucial. The heat generated is inspired by the game and not by a wish to make trouble.

This chapter started with a consideration of the strangeness of the Egyptian scene and of the essential friendliness and helpfulness of most Egyptians. It seems right, therefore, to finish not only this chapter but this whole contemplation of living Egypt with a few reflections on the simple image that best typifies both ancient and modern Egypt - surely that of the farmer in his field, ploughing with two oxen and a rather primitive plough. The small-scale cultivation of fields irrigated from water-channels, with the farmer's foot kicking aside the little earth dam, is unchanged. In his modern village life, discounting the disposable conveniences of modern living, the farmer has the same concerns and the same needs as his ancient counterpart. Success depends, as ever, on the equitable procession of the seasons, with crops and harvests following in regular succession. The disappearance of the inundation may be the greatest change in rural life since antiquity, and its final effects may be yet to be measured. The patient worker on the land has always been the one who has borne the brunt of life's trials in Egypt; it was he who in ancient times was periodically conscripted for public service; it was he who endured the injustice of the *corvée*; he built the pyramids and the Suez Canal. Equally it is the women of the villages who perform the multifarious tasks at home and in the fields; they are powerful in the family, guardians of traditional ways and customs, very often providing the moral strength of a household.

Rootedness in the soil of Egypt provides the stability and the possibility for continuity. When you ask an Egyptian where he or she comes from, you enquire after the *bilad*, the village. Egyptians may have become Cairenes by profession or habitation, but they will remain proud of their origins, in their *bilad*, in their land. When Egypt ceases to be a land of farmers, the change will be one of great loss. Its particularities and peculiarities are too precious to be submerged in the general tide of sameness that seeks to level life in all lands. Changes will always come, but in Egypt let us hope they will come from the strength of continuity, and not just from a wish to be like others, and therefore ordinary.

109 *opposite* A supreme royal portrait: the half life-size statue of the great conqueror King Tuthmosis III (Eighteenth Dynasty, c.1450 BC). Majesty and humanity are here combined with technical perfection (Luxor Museum, J2).

110 *overleaf* A view over Cairo at dusk from a minaret on the Bab Zuweila. In the distance is the mosque of Mohamed Ali on the Citadel.

Concise Chronology

For the earlier periods the dates used here are those found in J. Baines and J. Malek,
Atlas of Ancient Egypt, Oxford, 1978.

3000 BC ————————————————————————————————

Before c. 2920 BC	**PREDYNASTIC PERIOD** Egypt up to unification	
c. 2920-2649 BC	**EARLY DYNASTIC PERIOD** Dynasties I and II	
c. 2649-2150 BC	**OLD KINGDOM** Dynasties III-VI	
c. 2150-2040 BC	**FIRST INTERMEDIATE PERIOD** Dynasties VII-XI	

2000 BC ———— c. 2040-1700 BC ———— **MIDDLE KINGDOM** Dynasties XI-XIII

c. 1700-1550 BC	**SECOND INTERMEDIATE PERIOD** Dynasties XIII-XVII	
c. 1550-1070 BC	**NEW KINGDOM** Dynasties XVIII-XX	

1000 BC ———— c. 1070-712 BC ———— **LATE NEW KINGDOM** (now often called **THIRD INTERMEDIATE PERIOD**) Dynasties XXI-XXIV

712-332 BC	**LATE PERIOD** Dynasties XXV-XXX	
332-30 BC	**PTOLEMAIC PERIOD** Macedonian Greek rulers	

0 AD ———— 30 BC - 395 AD ———— **ROMAN PERIOD** Roman emperors

395-638 AD	**BYZANTINE PERIOD** Roman rule from Constantinople	

MUSLIM EGYPT

639-868 AD	Arab and Turkish governors
868-905 AD	Tulunid Dynasty
935-969 AD	Ikhshidid Dynasty

1000 AD ———— 969-1171 AD ———— Fatimid Dynasty

1171-1250 AD	Ayyubid Dynasty
1250-1517 AD	Mamluk Dynasties
1517-1798 AD	Ottoman rule
1798-1805 AD	Napoleonic invasion and aftermath
1805-1952 AD	Mohammed Ali and successors
1882-1922 AD	British occupation and protectorate
1922-1952 AD	Kingdom of Egypt
1952-	Revolution and Republic

Select Bibliography

Aldred, C., *The Egyptians*, London, 1984

Baines, J. and Malek, J., *Atlas of Ancient Egypt*, Oxford, 1978

Bell, H.I., *Egypt from Alexander the Great to the Arab Conquest*, Oxford, 1948

Biegman, N.H., *Egypt: Moulids, Saints, Sufis*, London, 1991

Bowman, A.K., *Egypt after the Pharaohs*, London, 1986

Butler, A.J., *The Ancient Coptic Churches of Egypt*, 2 vols, Oxford, 1884; new edn 1970

Butzer, K.W., *Early Hydraulic Civilization in Egypt*, Chicago and London, 1976

Cromer, Earl of (Evelyn Baring), *Modern Egypt*, 2 vols, London, 1908

Curzon, R. *Visits to the Monasteries in the Levant*, London, 1849; new edn 1983

Duff-Gordon, L., *Letters from Egypt*, London, 1865; new edn 1983

Fahry, A., *The Oases of Egypt*, I, *Siwa Oasis*, Cairo, 1973; II, *Bahriyah and Farafra Oases*, Cairo, 1974

Gardiner, A.H., *Egypt of the Pharaohs*, Oxford, 1962

Harris, J.R. (ed.), *The Legacy of Egypt*, Oxford, 1972

James, T.G.H., *Ancient Egypt. The Land and its Legacy*, London, 1988

Kees, H., *Ancient Egypt. A Cultural Topography*, London, 1961

KHS-Burmester, O.H.E., *A Guide to the Ancient Coptic Churches of Cairo*, Cairo, 1955

Lane, E.W., *An Account of the Manners and Customs of the Modern Egyptians*, London, 1835

Lane-Poole, S., *A History of Egypt in the Middle Ages*, London, 1901

Lichtheim, M., *Ancient Egyptian Literature*, 3 vols, Berkeley, Los Angeles, London, 1973-1980

Lucas, A., *Ancient Egyptian Materials and Industries*, 4th edn, ed. J.R.Harris, London, 1962

McPherson, J.W., *The Moulids of Egypt*, Cairo, 1941

Marlowe, J., *Anglo-Egyptian Relations 1800-1953*, London, 1954

Marsot, A.L.A., *Egypt in the Reign of Muhammed Ali*, Cambridge, 1984

Meinardus, O., *Christian Egypt, Ancient and Modern*, Cairo, 1977

Murnane, W.J., *The Penguin Guide to Ancient Egypt*, Harmondsworth, 1983

Russell, D., *Medieval Cairo and the Monasteries of the Wadi Natrun*, London, 1962

Vatikiotis, P.J., *The Modern History of Egypt*, London, 1969

Walters, C.C., *Monastic Archaeology in Egypt*, Warminster, 1974

Night falls over the Luxor Temple on the banks of the Nile.

Photographic Information

Most of Graham Harrison's photographs for this book were taken using a Wista
Field Camera with Schneider Super - Angulon 90mm f 5.6, Schneider Apo - Symmar
120mm f 5.6, Rodenstock Sironar - N 180mm f 5.6 and Schneider Apo - Symmar
210mm f 5.6 lenses. Film used was Kodak Ektachrome 100 Plus Professional
Readyload and Polaroid 64T Professional Chrome. Processing was by
Keishi Colour Ltd, Unit 15, 21 Wren Street, London WC1X OHF.

Index